Get A Hold Of Yourself

Trust your convictions, live your faith

 **STARRED REVIEW**

Get a Hold of Yourself: Trust Your Convictions, Live Your Faith
Xolani Kacela, Ph.D.
Xolani Kacela, 219 pages, (paperback) $16.99, 978-1-5136-6392-0
(Reviewed: September, 2020)

A Unitarian Universalist minister and chaplain for the New Mexico Air National Guard, Xolani Kacela shares how he went from a mixed religious background (the African Methodist Episcopal faith of his mother and the religious skepticism of his father) into a more stable, fulfilling life as a "spiritual humanist, meaning that **spiritual practice and study are vital to me, yet so are the works of philosophers, poets, scientists, and musicians.**" With daily practices such as prayer and meditation, spiritual journaling, and reconciliation, he believes anyone can grow from a life predicated on rules imposed from the outside to one built on a unique foundation of personal conviction.

Kacela defines people who have "a hold on themselves" as **those who can "trust the living spirit's promises and depend on sustenance from their faith community." Specifically, this requires a commitment to "sustaining relationships," to a faith community of one's own choosing, and to "regular spiritual practices." He gives a clear picture of several nurturing practices, with emphasis on how to cement them into our daily lives.**

Kacela's writing is slightly formal, which doesn't obscure his authenticity, warmth, and humor, but rather gives his book gravitas. He has mapped out a unique space here, a place between traditional religion and New Age spirituality. His own experience with congregational worship and spiritual aid bestows him credibility, and he illuminates this spiritual trail with sacred texts of all religions and writings of a wide variety of spiritual mentors, including the renowned civil rights activist and mystic **Howard Thurman.** The book includes a 13-page bibliography of resource material at its end.

The author believes his audience will be 24- to 37-year-old men who may have felt uncomfortable in a more traditional religion, as he once did. Yet, his ability to credibly and passionately convey the benefits of a life of faith and the steps by which to achieve it will enlighten anyone looking for a more fulfilling way to live.

Get A Hold Of Yourself

NOV 10

Posted by **Literary Titan**

(https://booklife.com/project/get-a-hold-of-yourself-
trust-your-faith-live-your-convictions-49168)

Get a Hold of Yourself by Xolani Kacela is an exploration into the development of one's personal
faith as a strong foundation for personal actualization and for interacting with others. The
author speaks from a Unitarian Universalist perspective, but highlights that the focus is not
necessarily on a specific religion but on the acknowledgement of the validity of faith practices. In
summary, everyone needs a basis of faith and whether that turns out to be Christian principles
or another religion, the author suggests that the individual should make this search a priority.

He explores what it means to have sustaining faith, exemplary faith, and the importance of
spiritual practices on one's faith journey. One of the main themes is that of independence and
coming to an individual place of strength and spiritual identity. That is what it means to truly get a
hold of one's self. The author explores different ways to come to this level of realization and
identity including

prayer, journaling and having a support community. He uses examples of faith leaders in his own
life and his own experiences to illustrate the principles suggested. He notes that the spiritual journey is
not necessarily a linear one but can include what he calls 'faith detours'. These detours are usually
not a departure from a main faith identity but are usually further explorations of other faith concepts.

The author makes the content general enough for many persons from different backgrounds to be able
to relate. He does so by emphasizing the results of having strong faith such as being able to withstand
the struggles of life and being less influenced by outside forces. It comes with great conviction and
without anxiety. It comes with developing an anti-fragile mentality. It is not a manual for
eliminating the struggles of life but a handbook for attempting to handle each situation as they arise
and bouncing back stronger than before being challenged. The reader can use the suggestions in each
chapter as a starting point for developing their faith on their own time and initiative. *Get a Hold of
Yourself* is an inspirational and thought-provoking book that explores faith with a unique perspective.

Pages: 221

Get A Hold Of Yourself

Xolani Kacela, Ph.D.

X to the k Publishing

This book is dedicated to my spouse, Tamara, who is the most loving person that I know.

I also dedicate this book to all people who live abundantly with their chosen faith as a primary source of navigation, and to those who respect the faiths of others different than their own as fully and equally true and viable for living.

Acknowledgements

This book has been a long time coming. I've had a few readers that I leaned on heavily throughout the process. I'll begin with Cindy Hull, Esq., whose insightful commentary was affirming and rigorous. Without her diligence and friendship, I wouldn't have persisted. Thanks to Phyllis Stern, my editor in NYC, who gave me confidence and assurance. Finally, a shout out to Rosemary Sneeringer for her editing smoothness and bringing it altogether in one voice.

Contents

GET A HOLD OF YOURSELF

Preface

Getting a hold of yourself is about learning how to let go of what other people say, including the old "should" you're ready to leave behind. Instead, it's time to rely on your convictions, especially when it comes to your concept of spirituality.

Trusting your convictions in the spiritual realm leads you to greater personal and emotional freedom, allowing more joy in your life.

You will realize that you have your beliefs, and others have theirs, yet all of us are capable of living out those beliefs without infringing upon one another. This results in more peace in your inner spiritual world, the ability to live in harmony with others and to dwell in the grace of the divine—however you define that.

While getting a hold of yourself won't free you from daily frustrations or a divisive and partisan environment, it does provide you with important tools to self-soothe amid differing points of view. Differences don't have to be divisive. They don't have to become "a thing," unless you choose so.

Getting a hold of yourself is about learning how to let go of what other people say, including the old "should" you're ready to leave behind. Instead, it's time to rely on your convictions, especially when it comes to your concept of spirituality.

We always have new choices to activate peace and harmony, even when the culture can lure us into frustration, anger, and anxiety. When you're able to get a hold of yourself (or, as some people call it, sovereignty over your mind, heart, and thoughts), it makes all the difference in the world. To be in self-sovereignty, where the greater self is in charge of all the other parts of you is to be in harmony with oneself and the world.

Why trust me? I, too, was once embroiled in my anger and anxiety. Especially in the arena of faith and belief. I've had deep roots in various faith traditions, including the African Methodist Episcopal Church (AME), Baptist congregations, and lifelong exposure to humanist and atheist thought—quite a wide spectrum. What was right and what was wrong with those institutions? My judgments made me even more spiritually insecure and in need of more confidence.

After years of study, various spiritual practices, and finding a community to support you can provide even more than you're searching for. While working with spiritual mentors, I learned the value of community. Our own-rooted convictions can help us live a holistic life, but I've found that it's so much richer with a community.

Introduction

As a child, my mother whispered to me in one ear while my father murmured in the other. The religious part of my upbringing came from my mother; the non-religious came from my father. My mother was more assertive about teaching me to follow in her path while my father was more passive, allowing me to slide along, occasionally letting me know he didn't subscribe to my mother's belief system.

Looking back, I only belonged to a spiritual community by default. My upbringing told me that church was the right thing to do on Sunday mornings, which I attended for most of my life. Fortunately, I had just enough of my father's doubt and disbelief to realize there were more ways to spend my time when Sunday rolled around. Did I feel a level of guilt when I didn't show up at church? Yes. But it wasn't until I was well into my adulthood that my convictions began to evolve and come into full relief.

I realized I could trust my truths about religion and spirituality, let go of the guilt, and live my life on my terms. It took me about forty years, or the majority of my life, to "come to my senses" about my spiritual life. This is why I am writing this book. I don't want you to spend your life always trying, but ending up in circles.. You can begin the process right now, at this moment. I will teach you how to use the wisdom that is already inside yourself, and to trust your own convictions, living them as fully as possible.

I am an advocate of lifelong learning. I believe ongoing personal, professional, and spiritual development has no substitute and can take us further along on our path to wisdom. This book encourages deep engagement with various traditions. It is a wonderful companion on your journey of faith.

How can I teach you about living your convictions of faith? Who am I?

Back to mother and father's tug of war and clashing sides of the belief spectrum. Although I'd managed to pull myself out of those competing universes from time to time, I later realized both parents were sources of truth and the right principles for living. One was as equally valid as the other. I also recognized many perspectives in between, to the right and left of them. I ended up being a mixture of many sources of wisdom, even creating some of my own.

I now consider myself a spiritual humanist, meaning that spiritual practice and study are vital to me, yet so are the works of philosophers, poets, scientists, and musicians. I maintain a broad appreciation for the life of the mind and the soul, regarding both sacred and secular paths that enlighten me. Personal growth is valid and life-affirming to me. In my professional life, I am a Unitarian Universalist (UU) minister.

I understand there are many paths in a life of faith. Most are long and circuitous. These paths cover a lot of territory, determined by the sum of the seeker's knowledge, the intention of their practice, and a host of other factors. Within most paths of faith, however, some seem to have reached a pinnacle of wisdom and experience, and often serve as role models for others who follow in their footsteps.

A Typical Faith Journey or Detour

Many people who aspire to live a happy and fulfilling life are rooted in some sort of spiritual community. They grow up listening to sermons about what makes one a good person or what does not. The characteristics of good people are typically based on a certain belief system, meaning a person can't be "good" unless they promise to adopt those beliefs. Additionally, the culture around them communicates other sets of standards regarding what "success" looks like. Together, these beliefs and standards are what many people strive for.

The problem is that when you buy into others' beliefs and standards, you set yourself up for failure, disappointment, guilt, and shame when you fall short. The church and synagogue are especially good at perpetuating beliefs and standards, and insisting we abide by them perfectly. But none of us can do it. None of us! We must learn how to put those beliefs and standards in perspective to get a hold of ourselves. Otherwise, you'll find yourself constantly making faith detours instead of moving forward on your journey.

Dante's Story

The following story illustrates the circuitous route of two people whom I encountered in a Christian congregation. I'd like to emphasize that while these two examples have a Christian orientation, my aim is broader. These experiences could happen to people of any faith or religious tradition. And they do.

Regarded as a person of deep and strong faith, Dante walked down the aisle one Sunday morning and confessed to feeling distant from God, far away from the spiritual contentment he once had known.[1] He wanted to rededicate his life to the faith of his youth and his deepest yearnings. After sharing this, the congregation chanted their "amends," acknowledging that they understood what Dante had been experiencing, supporting his rededication to his faith. Everyone smiled, beaming with joy, as the minister thanked God for wanting to turn his life over to Christ.

Here was a man of thirty-five years who was anything but centered and in the depth of his faith. I was astonished. How could a person who was so involved in church (indeed a spiritual role model) feel he'd slipped so far that he needed to start over from scratch? For a minute, I thought this was a put-on. But unwilling to judge him, I went along with his wishes.

On another occasion, a close friend, Debra, had made the same confession. Again, I was baffled. What was I missing? These were people who appeared to be giants in their faith. Yet, before the congregation, they expressed feeling disconnected from God.

Later, I asked Debra about her public assertion. She told me she'd lost her close connection with God, feeling her life was purposeless and meaningless. She felt as if she'd been doing something wrong that needed correcting. By rededicating her life to the church and recommitting to pay more attention to her spiritual life, she intended to regain what she had lost. She wanted to feel hopeful and confident again that God loved her and that she was living faithfully to her core religious convictions.

---

[1] All cases are composites or fictitious and have been used with permission.

For Debra, like other devout people of many faiths, regaining a sense of "putting God first" in her life would change how she felt. By following God's commandments and trusting him in all ways, this was a shorthanded way of living prayerfully, studying scripture, attending services regularly, and participating in a faith community.

After some reflection, Debra and Dante's decision began to make sense to me. Something essential to faith development was happening in people's lives that hadn't been explained in typical Sunday sermons during that period of my life. The simple "trust and believe" formula wasn't panning out. There's a middle ground that people encountered once they began living out their faith commitments (which wasn't mapped out). So, when people found themselves in uncharted terrain, they blamed their lack of faith instead of their lack of training in how to maneuver life using the implements of faith. Simply said, they were stuck.

Though I first recognized this interaction between faith and growth in a Christian congregation (at the time I was training to be a United Methodist minister), I have come to see this as a universal pattern that spans the breadth of many spiritual paths. I hear similar groans now amongst my UU ministerial colleagues and parishioners. I have read about such patterns of faith development in various journals and newspapers, and see the pattern taking place in popular art-house films. It is all around us, but few see it.

I sense that people are: subscribing to communal beliefs, trying to incorporate them into their lives, falling short (as we all do at times) then, feeling bad about themselves and starting over again, knowing it wasn't anyone's fault.

We're all doing what we've been taught is right. It's human nature to follow the path of those who go before us—until—we find another path that suits us better.

I believe that you, and people such as Debra and Dante, deserve better when it comes to their spiritual lives. Everyone ought to be able to trust their values and convictions, even when they differ from their culture, or the synagogue, mosque, or church. If your beliefs happen to coincide with what you've been taught, that is fine, too. Just remember to trust yourself when you feel bereft or on shaky and unfamiliar ground. Perhaps it is about going deeper into faith, meditation, contemplation, or spending more time doing what one loves.

Years later during my work as a hospice chaplain, I encountered another type of spiritual personality—someone who spoke with deep confidence about his or her life of faith. This is a different type of story from that of Debra and Dante—a story of deep knowledge, wisdom, and a relationship with the powers of the universe. This personality was unflappable, even in hard times.

While working on my doctoral dissertation, I came up with a phrase to describe people who'd built well-developed faith. I called them *faith exemplars*. Their faith exemplified, or epitomized, a life filled with spiritual practices, sustaining relationships, and a supportive community of faith. While I still believe that description is accurate, it is too narrow for today's times. We need a different term that speaks clearly about self-transformation.

Getting a hold of yourself speaks to a process. Those with exemplary faith have gotten a hold of themselves, living life based on their convictions and values. Their spiritual practices are part of their inner and outer world, and they belong to diverse communities (cherishing relationships with diverse people) that nourish their spirit.

This book is meant to help people who are searching for a well-rounded life but do not know how to achieve it. Like Debra and Dante, we all can turn our lives around by learning to "exemplify" convictions and values held so dearly, without the negative feelings so often attached to the process. As you love yourself inside and out, be sure to be patient with yourself.

More on Who This Book was Written For

Although this book was written for persons of various religious and faith traditions, it is based on my Unitarian Universalist (UU) faith identity. As a Unitarian Universalist minister who has served in congregations, both large and small, I have observed many members and friends living a tentative spiritual life. They thoroughly enjoy participating in the faith community and often make astonishing contributions, but often are unable to articulate their faith identity or their place along the spectrum of faith.

Many Unitarian Universalists are quite adept at expressing what they dislike about the religion of their youth and why they departed that faith. Their stories come bursting out, along with the bad memories. Yet, when it comes to speaking with the same passion about their current faith convictions, spiritual theology, or life philosophy, they are rather reluctant or timid. There is nothing wrong with this, even if one has no firmly developed convictions. Yet, the deepest hope is that being more intentional and secure about your life of faith—whatever it may be—will help you articulate your own faith identity with more ease and assurance.

I've learned that becoming secure in your faith identity is a complicated process, one that is not necessarily presented on a Friday night or Sunday morning, although one may find glimpses of it there. Realistically, it is a continuous process that happens over time. The more you are committed to getting a hold of yourself and the more intentional you are, the more natural it becomes. This process is akin to a "lifelong learner," a person who commits themselves to ongoing growth, achievement, and well-being.

I have found that readers of this book will be millennials or at the top range of Generation Z. In 2020, this would be a twenty-four to thirty-seven year old. In 2025, this group will be twenty-eight to forty-two years old. Although many women will read this book, I'm finding that more men are seeking new paths after following traditional religion and looking for more inclusive fellowship.

Men, do you wish you were more confident, wise, and fulfilled in your life? Would you trust your instincts and walk into a crowded room knowing what you say is deeply profound? Even more important, are you able to trust your convictions, your values, and lean on your own experience? These are the components that make up who you are. If so, then I suggest getting a hold of yourself.

This means stop worrying and fretting. At this moment, you probably have the foundations of a great life, leaning on your principles and your faith as your cornerstone. How-ever, trusting those convictions, putting them into practice.

SECTION I

What it Means to Have Sustaining Faith

This section explains what it means to possess faith and be capable of withstanding the very forces in life that often break down our hope and sense of progression, leaving us despondent and searching for answers.

Chapter 1

Understanding Sustaining Faith

When we use the term faith, we are referring to a gift from the Spirit of Life, a gift to humanity that is developed through spiritual practices and ongoing relationships often formed in your family, religious or spiritual communities, and indeed, wherever you find yourself. This spiritual gift shapes the course of your life and guides you in yielding actively to a transcendent source whose presence and promises will bring hope to your life. This is our definition in the most general terms, describing what people aspire to in their spiritual journey. I believe that we are born with a survival instinct that we inherently trust to lead us forward. This nascent faith grows as we intentionally attend to the components of faith as we conceive them. You might consider such intention as a minimum requirement, or baseline of action, for a conscious, well-lived life.

But when we speak of a deep, sustaining faith, the emphasis shifts from *the knowledge of* faith to the *capacity to use* faith to meet life's ongoing challenges. People who possess this use their faith actively. For them, faith is more than a dormant set of beliefs and convictions. It is something that propels them forward and activates their desire to live fully each day. Such people intuitively know that the future is open-ended and full of mystery, surprise, and things they couldn't have anticipated. Yet they are confident that they will get through it, and, if nothing else, be able to withstand, or take on, finishing each day with productive outcomes.

An example can illuminate how faith can emerge over a brief period and begin taking hold in a person's life. A parishioner named Janice had gone through a difficult divorce, and two years later she came to see me. For her, losing her marriage, significant relationships, and most of her material possessions resulted in starting all over in many areas of her life, especially with her faith journey. At times, she felt she'd abandoned all she believed in by going through with the divorce. Her dream of being a devoted wife who answered the sacred call to married life, her obligation to teach her children lessons of faith, and most importantly, living out her most cherished spiritual values in a community of faith, meant, to her, that she was no longer living a meaningful life.

During our time together in pastoral counseling, I offered Janice a space to reflect upon how her faith may have sustained her over the previous two years following her divorce. It turned out that she was agnostic and had cultivated a practice of reading poetry in the morning online. She began remembering how her occasional yoga practice had put her in contact with her inner strength and kept her in touch with people she enjoyed seeing. Gradually, she began pulling together the various threads of faith that her identity had slipped below the radar but were still active. By the end of the sessions, she emerged with a resolution that, indeed, her faith life was still alive and sustaining her. Though her losses were real, and nothing could bring them back, Janice gradually regained her confidence in herself and began creating a new plan for her future. This would include reestablishing important relationships, starting new ones, and significantly, revising her self-image as a divorced woman. One with more life ahead of her than before. She was more confident than ever that her faith (agnosticism) was sufficient to guide her forward.

Like Janice, people who have a hold of themselves grow to know instinctively, by practicing spiritual disciplines, that they can trust the living spirit's promises and depend on sustenance from their faith community.

Several qualities contribute to this faith perspective:

a positive outlook on life

the ability to deal with the struggles of life

maintaining a non-anxious presence

and creating a future vision

Let us examine each of these in detail.

A Positive Outlook on Life

I particularly remember meeting a "faith giant" named John. Prior to entering the nursing home, the attending nurse and physician alerted me that the patient, John's mother, was fading quickly. I entered the room, hoping that someone from the family would be present so I could learn about the patient and offer appropriate pastoral care. But I hadn't prepared myself for the powerful force awaiting me in the room. The patient's son, John, was standing at the bedside looking at his mother. After I introduced myself and asked how he was holding up, he responded astounded with joy, "I'm doing fabulously!"

I was taken aback and asked him how he could be so enthusiastic in light of his mother's approaching death. He said, "Because I know God!" He went on to describe his faith journey with an amazing lack of reticence. He was not only positive, but he also radiated confidence that confirmed his faith stood at the center of his life and his mother's. While listening to John's testimony, I couldn't help but wonder if he were in some form of deep denial by not acknowledging his mother's death. After more conversations, it emerged that his mother had, indeed, lived a long and fulfilling life, and through a slow grieving process he had accepted that her end time had come. He remained unwavering in his conviction that his faith would sustain him as he contemplated the meaning of his mother's death and his life ahead without her.

This positive outlook drives the faith-based attitude towards life that "God will work it out." It signals the deep-seated conviction that whatever happens, we can trust the spirit to guide the situation. People who have a hold of themselves approach life realistically and without the grandiose expectations that characterize many pie-in-the-sky faith paradigms. As scripture reminds us, "The rain falls on the just and unjust." There is no rhyme or reason for either occurrence, so it is wise to be prepared for either outcome.

Exemplary faith has a quality similar to the power of positive thinking, an outlook pioneered by Norman Vincent Peale. But mature faith, while hoping for the best, acknowledges a range of outcomes. Assuming a can-do attitude adds a touch of lightness to faith. We need not be deeply serious all the time to have extraordinary faith.

When I first began encountering examples of strong faith in the hospice setting, their positive outlook and sunny disposition were stunning and intriguing. Most other patients and families were subdued in their emotional expression and the prevailing atmosphere was quiet, low-key, with a rather severe undertone. After I spent more time there, it seemed that this limited range of feelings and mental dispositions had dampened the mood and outlook of the dying patients. This way of being was understandable. After all, many patients and families were simply not in the frame of mind for much more than resignation or despair.

Dealing With the Vicissitudes of Life

In the story above, John's positive demeanor, even in the face of death, demonstrates another capacity that arises from sustaining faith: the ability to face life's difficulties head-on. M. Scott Peck's famous opening sentence from *The Road Less Traveled* is "Life is difficult." Once we realize this, he argues, that fact no longer matters. Harnessing the capacity to yield and depend on the gifts of transcendence is so needed when confronting death and dying. This means gathering the strength and trust to keep moving forward when uncertainty, despair, and possible gloomy outcomes litter the landscape of life.

Having sustained faith means knowing that life is made up of both joyous occasions and disheartening difficulties. For one thing, human decision-making is faulty, and many outcomes do not work out as planned. With an error in judgment here and there, the best plans may fall apart. Any half-hearted baseball fan knows that even the best hitters have a batting average under .300; indeed, managing three out of ten attempts to connect with the ball is considered excellent. In the life of faith, we hope for better than a .300 batting average, but we understand that the average may represent a best-case scenario. Exemplary faith prepares people to effectively manage their lives and personal affairs, even when the odds are low. A low batting average does not mean that God's gift of faith has failed us or that we have failed to live out our faith commitments. It only means that normal life has its ups and downs and we must continue to march on.

Immature faith often does not hold up under similar circumstances. You may recall the early days in your life of faith, usually characterized by a decision to "wake up" from a former way of living or existing in the world. For example, a person encounters a Buddhist spiritual teacher and is prompted to explore what it means to become Buddhist. We might call this a "conversion experience." Early on in this journey, the newly-minted Buddhist decides to follow the eightfold path and devote some time each day to meditation. She may incorporate reading scriptures from the Gita into her daily routine. As these changes become routine, life will gradually expand as she sees her daily experience through a new lens of Buddhist teachings. Over time, she will begin interpreting her life through this new faith. And with the help of her teacher, her faith shall grow and begin solving problems with her new spiritual knowledge.

This move to explore a new faith in itself represents a significant milestone. To get there, typically we've passed through childhood, adolescence, and early adulthood—when we relied on life and faith experiences passed down from your parents, peers, and institutions, such as schools, houses of worship, and universities. As the faith theorist James Fowler makes clear, in these earlier stages of a faith journey, our concept of faith and meaning-making relies heavily on "External authority." In the earlier stages of the faith journey, people may treat difficult life situations as existential crises that may deflate their faith all together, where their faith had always been seen as a protective shield against life's circumstances. When things do go wrong, those with undeveloped faith are more likely to turn against, rather than turn within themselves and to others for strength. They may view themselves as bad people or being unworthy of that transcendent love. In contrast, exemplars understand the world is as it is, meaning that some things will not end in our favor no matter how hard we pray, meditate, or trust in the divine. But that is the nature of life and not the result of our personal failings.

Faith increases as a result of an intentional life—from the inside out. I call it "Inside out" because, as Fowler notes, an "Internal locus of authority that predominates" in our world resides at this level of faith. In other words, we rely on our own sense of calm, assurance, and confidence, not necessarily attending to the events of the world. We can be steadfast in our beliefs and not weighed down by the world. For those in sovereignty and high spirits (no matter what is going on) their high vibration reverberates good things back to them. Those who are always complaining or in fear will encounter exactly that in the outside world. Though world events may prompt us to reexamine our core narrative, the foundation of exemplary faith stands strong because it originates from within us.

Non-anxious Presence

In pastoral counseling circles, the term *non-anxious presence* refers to a caregiver's ability to remain calm amid volatile family systems. The purpose, says Rabbi Edwin Freidman in his seminal work, *Generation to Generation*, is "To take maximum responsibility for one's own destiny and emotional being. It can be measured by the breadth of one's repertoire of responses when confronted with crisis." This manner of being is important because conflicts and crises are always looming, especially for individuals, families, and communities of faith where the constellation of personalities often induces anxiety. In anxious systems, homeostatic forces maintain anxiety by resisting change. When mature personalities emerge to resolve crises, less mature personalities tend to resist such change, and instead, act to bring the system to a state of lower functioning to maintain balance.

For example, a client, Derrick, reported going home for a family reunion. Upon his arrival, an aunt who had been central to the family system became deathly ill. Many family members were upset over the aunt's inability to participate in reunion activities. Some lobbied to cancel the entire event to stay with her at the hospital. Derrick, like many of the others who had traveled several hundred miles to be at the reunion, recognized the importance of standing up to his family during this emotional meltdown. He chose to exert leadership. He reminded key family members of their collective triumphs in the past, and how God had helped them weather many storms. Eventually, the emotional climate of the family began to calm down (and function less anxiously) and the planned events went on. The family revised a schedule to make sure the aunt received proper care and attention.

Had Derrick not maintained a non-anxious presence in the midst of the family upheaval, more relational damage may have resulted. For example, I have seen families (who professed deep trust in God's benevolence) completely abandon their sense of religious community and spiritual practices in the face of hardship. Family members have turned against one another—even the children against their parents. Derrick's resolve to take responsibility for himself (his thoughts, feelings, and actions in response to those around him) enabled him to continue creating the narrative, or story of his faith, that he had previously chosen for himself. Moreover, his faith was "at the ready," capable of stimulating change within the family system at the moment it was needed.

People with mature, sustaining faith can expect to be challenged to forgo their calm demeanor by characteristically anxious people—as Derrick was challenged by his family. There will always be situations that call us to take a stand as a result of our faith experience and to maintain our serenity. The person able to remain calm, stable, and endure life's challenges is more likely to develop mature faith.

Howard Thurman offers us a mindset to hold on to the inner calm needed throughout life: "Man's journey is hazardous because the world in which he lives is grounded in order and held intact by an inner and irresistible logic, by laws that, in one vast creative sweep, encompass the infinite variety of the universe and give life its stability, but at the same time make living anywhere, at any time, a dramatic risk for any particular unit of life." By adopting this way of seeing the world, we can be less anxious. That is, by acting "as if" Thurman's prescription is true, as they say in Alcoholics Anonymous, we can try on this mindset for ourselves. You may ask, "Why would I want to adopt the practices of AA?" One, because it has proven to produce the desired results, and two, because many consider AA's practices a form of secular spirituality.

Future Vision

"Where there is no vision, the people perish, but happy is the one who heeds instruction." (Proverbs 29:18). A life without vision is likely to be unhappy, unfulfilling, and enmeshed in despair. With vision, with a goal in sight, the human animal is driven into the future. Vision is the fuel for pursuing our passion giving our lives meaning. In this sense, vision is that thing "hoped for" found at the core of faith when people have "taken a hold" of themselves.

A gold miner digging in the earth for a vein of gold imagines himself digging and digging, and finally finding that sweet spot. Until he finds it, he is motivated by the vision of success. He envisions the joy that he'll have, the fame and fortune accompanying his feat, the pleasure that he'll feel, and of course, a more prosperous life. Each of these components engenders in the miner a vision of a better life, one filled with more purpose than his present situation. The faith journey is similar.

The spiritual practices and relationships that make up the faith process are similar, with each chisel of the rock being akin to a practice that strengthens our faith. We're not certain that we'll discover a nugget, but we continue as if we are determined. Those growing in the life of faith imagine themselves living better with a deep, resilient faith than without it. Therefore, they apply themselves daily to their tasks, while ensuring that their vision becomes a reality. Their vision is filled with images of realizing the holy promises of a life transformed.

Their vision is filled with images of realizing the holy promises of a life transformed.

Each of these qualities, like "fruits of the spirit," develops over time as a person makes their way through life. In many cases, these personality traits develop without direct, conscious effort. While individuals may consciously attend to their spiritual lives, they are not thinking "This will lead me to become an exemplar." They are merely following their own disciplined path or one that they inherited from others because that helps them accomplish the future they envision.

Chapter 2

A Broad Description of Faithing

For centuries, in the West, the Bible has provided the classic meaning of faith. Hebrews 11 describes faith as "The assurance of things hoped for, the evidence of things not seen." The noun, faith, describes an inner stance, or way of being, that governs how we engage the present and future. The verb, "faithing," transforms the Hebrews' perspective into an action or way of living out our spiritual lives. Persons of faith take an active role in their faithing process; exemplary or mature faith does not just happen on its own. The Apostle Paul recognized that all persons of faith are not immediately exemplars. For those who were infants in the faith, he said, "I fed you with milk, not solid food, for you were not ready for solid food" (1 Cor. 3.2). None of us comes into the world, or the life of faith for that matter, able to eat "solid food." Faithing is an ongoing activity that requires intentional effort if you are to grow and develop *assurance* and *conviction* of those things hoped for and unseen.

These efforts focus on relationships, spiritual practices, and participating in a caring community. As you will soon discover, this process of transformation is ongoing or evolving. In other words, faithing is a lifelong journey. Sometimes you may feel as though you've backslid or regressed, but don't let that derail you. Simply pay attention to that faithful feeling and continue on your way.

Faithing as a Verb

Faithing only indirectly refers to belief. In other words, it is less concerned with the content of people's belief systems (although that is important) and more concerned with one's spiritual identity, so that the implements of their faith can be attained. The well-known scholar of religion, Wilfred Cantwell Smith, once remarked that *to believe* meant to "Hold dear." He refers to holding one's belief in the divine dear to one's heart. Holding on to one's beliefs can transform faith into an *activity* of the heart.

But that is not all.

Once a belief is held dear, we must do something with it for it to become realized in our daily lives. A belief that is simply held dear, treasured, or saved for a later time is unlikely to leave us changed—much like our body remains unchanged if we only think about exercise but don't do it. Faithing is about bringing about change and deepening our understanding of what can be *done* with our gifts from our transcendent source of life. Or, in this case, the gift of the living spirit in action.

This book does not discourage beliefs. After all, belief is the core of much religious and spiritual identity. Here, I include people who practice secular faith, which is often left out in various forms of social justice action. For example, we are in the midst of massive changes in the earth's climate. Many secular faith-affiliated people are advocating for governmental support on regulations that limit the effect of human activity on our environment. However, it is not enough to solely advocate for change. More definitive action is needed, such as voting for legislators who support such regulations, including buying smaller cars and making our homes more efficient. These are some means of translating belief into action.

Faithing as Evolution

Your faith *evolves*. Where you begin is not where you will end up. How you practice your religious life as a child is unlikely to be the same when you enter adulthood. As we age, our understanding of the world around us ebbs and flows. While some change happens slowly, some occurs rapidly, depending on your readiness to accept and embrace what is going on at any moment in your life. Certain events will induce more change than others.

And without warning, you will find yourself capable of taking a leap of faith and creating a new understanding of who you are, what life means, and what your assignment in life is. As a result of these momentous events, your faith also changes to match and accommodate your new understanding.

Take as an example, what happened as a result of the events of September 11, 2001. On an individual level, many persons of faith began to reflect and reassess what the attacks meant about the role religion played in their lives. Suddenly, Americans found themselves living in a land that was vulnerable to what seemed like unknown, foreign forces of evil. This knowledge pushed many of us to alter our lives to adapt to the new reality. Many rediscovered church, synagogue, or other communities of belonging, and recommitted to living more prayerfully, spiritually and aligned with their core values. Before 9-11, many people viewed the role of faith in their lives one way; after 9-11, that was changed to another way. Adapting to new modes of living and perspectives on the world demonstrates the evolution of faith.

I, for one, realized how fragile life actually is. Watching the towers come down on TV, I immediately grasped how quickly a life (or lives) can dissipate into thin air. What begins as a "normal" day can quickly go sideways and turn into a nightmare. The 9-11 attacks brought my awareness front and center about something I'd already known, but wasn't acting on with any expediency: life is time-limited, therefore, make every day count. Live with purpose as a habit.

I recall having conversations with people who interpreted the events as the "end times" and the fulfillment of prophecy. Others saw it as justification to point fingers at people they felt culpable for our collective misfortune as a nation. Those grounded in deep faith and strong moral conviction continued to live out those perspectives and broaden their understanding of the world to match the new reality. One example that I appreciated were those communities in New York that began interfaith work between churches and mosques. Rather than succumb to hatred, those communities continued to see the good and join ranks to mend hearts, assisting those in need.

When we insist on using old paradigms that no longer work or have lost their power to change our lives, we invite frustration and unnecessary suffering. As adults, do we pray the same old prayer that we prayed as a child? Not usually. Then why do we continue to keep the same spiritual practices we learned years ago even when they no longer yield the desired spiritual results? Using old, outdated paradigms is a sign of resisting the evolving nature of faith. Why do we do it? Sometimes it's because we're not being challenged to look at the world differently. But more often than not, it's because of the human tendency to remain in a comfortable space and keep things the same. At its worst, resistance to the evolutionary nature of faith can stagnate personal growth.

Church hopping is a symptom of resisting our faith's evolution. This is a practice of going from church to church seeking a new level of religious and spiritual fulfillment. People feel if they can just find the right church or the right preacher who knows how to bring the "right word," our spiritual lives will blossom or go to the "next level." People with liberal traditions, such as Unitarians, may not use the phrase, "Bring the word," but we too, are in love with words! In such cases, if the preacher is poetic or scholarly enough, then church-hopping may stop. Invariably, church hopping ends in dismal failure because the root cause of the spiritual unrest is internal, not external. We resist the evolution of our faith to our peril. Because churches tend to teach *what* to think and believe vs. *how* to act upon thoughts and beliefs for our faith evolution, those who church hop will always find dissatisfaction.

A neighbor from my distant past was a Baptist when we had first met. He seemed to enjoy talking about their services and how uplifting their message was for him. Gradually, I noticed he was going to church with less regularity. He remarked that things were "changing" at his congregation and he wasn't "being fed" by the minister anymore. He switched to a church of a different denomination. A non-denominational congregation, because the minister preached the "true word," meaning a more faithful interpretation of the scriptures. Soon, there was an incident at that church involving the minister, so the neighbor felt he'd been duped, believing this minister was "like all the others," meaning not to be trusted. He concluded it was time to take a break from church and do his own thing. In all likelihood, what my neighbor was searching for in a faith community was there all along. He was not at a place in his faith evolution to connect with people in the churches he encountered or the messages he'd heard.

Instead of moving from one church to another in our search for deeper spiritual meaning, church or synagogue hoppers can begin shifting their understanding to an evolutionary one. As long as we expect a new church or pastor or rabbi to do the work of faithing for us, growth will not occur. *Each person must do the work of faithing individually* and *from the inside out.* The spirit of unity gives us the motivation and volition to change, but we *need* to bring about change by actively engaging our faith.

A Voluntary Effort

The evolutionary nature of taking a hold of your faith goes hand-in-hand with its voluntary nature. We previously discussed resistance and the human tendency to continue doing things the same old way.

People with mature faith release their old ways that no longer work, choosing instead new ways of embracing the future that life promises.

When we voluntarily participate in the evolution of our faith, we make a conscious decision to act, fully aware of our choice to do so. As Thomas Moore writes in his book, *A Faith of Our Own*, "Our faith life is about transcending, going beyond. It's more a verb than a noun."

Therefore, we take voluntary action knowing that our spiritual growth depends on our willingness to allow ourselves to evolve. This critical awareness is vital. It entails paying attention to what our faith experience is telling us at any given moment.

There is an expression, "Healthy people speak up." Likewise, faith exemplars speak up when they need to act. This voluntary act of allowing and even inviting the development of faith to run its course becomes intuitive, or second nature.

Finding Opportunities to Evolve

We look for opportunities to evolve our faith. We don't passively wait for life to run its course, hoping for the best. An active life of faith demands that we keep our hearts and minds open to God's cues and that growth occurs. We keep an eye on the landscape of faith in search of ways to push ourselves out of our comfort zones and into new territory.

Think of how Ruth and Naomi have come out of their comfort zones. As the story goes, because of a famine in the country called Moab, Naomi and her two daughters-in-law set out for Judah because "she had heard that the Lord has taken note of his people and given them food" (1.6). Knowing the hardships that lay ahead on their journey, Naomi encouraged both younger women to return to their biological families unburdened by her. Despite Naomi's strong admonition to return, Ruth used her faithing "veto power" and objected to Naomi's request saying, "Do not urge me to leave you, to turn back and not follow you. For wherever you go, I will go; wherever you lodge, I will lodge; your people shall be my people, and your God my God." (v 1.16). Ruth willingly proceeded into new territory. She and Naomi used the journey back to Judah as an opportunity to evolve and test their faith.

When they embarked upon their journey, they had no idea how they would provide for themselves. In ancient cultures, unaccompanied women were quite vulnerable and relied heavily on the goodness and kindness of those they encountered for their livelihood, for protection, food, drink, and shelter. Ruth and Naomi had to trust in something grander than they could imagine, to look out for them and show them a path. Ruth, knowing her mother-in-law to be an older, wiser woman, put her faith in Naomi's wisdom and guidance, which she followed faithfully. Ruth sought out Naomi's brother-in-law, as Naomi instructed, and presented herself to him, trusting that he would respond compassionately and according to the faith customs laid down over generations. And as a man of integrity and compassion, he responded accordingly and took the two women under his care and provided for them.

This story depicts exemplary faith on many levels. The two women knew from experience that Jehovah, as God is called in the Jewish scriptures, would be there throughout the journey, watching over them, offering protection, and fulfilling Jehovah's promises. The famine presented an opportunity to evolve their faith and put it to the test. They could easily have remained in Moab with their families, but they chose to pay attention to the Divine's message and respond according to their deepest convictions.

Many of us have faced similar forks in the road ourselves. A job we love turns sour, a new job opportunity presents itself, but it's across the country, away from our family and loved ones. We have a choice to make. A romantic connection develops over the internet, but the love interest does not live nearby, or perhaps does not meet all the qualifications of our "ideal match." A frequent "close-to-home" faith occurrence is when an adult child reaches a fork in the road and asks to return home to their parents. Each scenario tests our faith. There are no easy answers. Do we read this as the universe placing a call upon our future, and proceed into the unknown to live out our faith convictions? Or do we go with what we consider a safe route? There are often no easy answers, but I want to encourage you to move forward with your faith as a guide.

But let's not confuse looking for opportunities to evolve our faith with randomly assigning a divine maker of these events. While our faith may grow as a result of reflecting on God's ability to influence outcomes, this has a passive quality that doesn't necessarily stretch or challenge our faith. The active faith referenced here is future-oriented. Also, looking to the past for cause and effect is not the same as looking for opportunities to evolve our faith in the present. Pointing out that God, or the divine, caused a series of events is an exercise in hindsight. Evolving one's faith requires a leap into the future.

The Art of Remembering

Another resource for faithing is to remember lessons from the past so our history becomes a source of trustworthy knowledge. Many religious traditions encourage spiritual practices steeped in remembering. Scripture reads, "These commandments that I give you today are to be upon your hearts. Impress them on your children. Talk about them when you sit at home and when you walk along the road, when you lie down and when you get up." (Deuteronomy 6.6) This text instructs parents to discuss divine acts with their children as a means of forming memories that will sustain them over time.

Our culture puts a premium on data and various forms of information. The information is transmitted quickly, used up, and soon forgotten. It takes much more effort to remember the faith lessons from our past and those of our ancestors. In the sacred verses, parents are called to pause and tell stories. This takes time and energy. But the act of repetition reinforces the stories and the truths they intended to instill. Eventually, the stories become a part of the collective consciousness of those who listen. Rather than listening and discarding the content of such stories, sustaining faith requires an intentional effort to save and preserve these narratives.

Models of faith are masters of remembering. They can recall their personal stories of God's action in their lives and skillfully appropriate the stories passed down to them by their predecessors. Leaders from the civil rights era in the fifties and sixties were known for telling stories of liberation from the Bible as sources of faith and strength. In his book, *Our Home is Over Jordan*, pastoral theologian Homer Ashby, Jr. cites the Exodus story as the significant memory conjured during the struggle. He argues, "Through the story of the plight of the Israelites, African Americans could see their own experience and thereby gain an interpretive perspective on that experience." In effect, the leaders adopted the trustworthy exodus story and preached it to the masses as a means of galvanizing the freedom movement—which was an exodus of its own.

We have witnessed former president Barack Obama call upon his memories of his father's life as a source of strength in his own life. His book on the topic, *Dreams From My Father*, became a bestseller and allowed millions of people all over the world to connect with his story, and ultimately, his vision of government and community. Obama used his faith story to discuss difficult subjects, such as race, his relationship with his former pastor, the Rev. Jeremiah Wright, and most importantly, to galvanize the nation in his run for the presidency. Many Americans, especially

African Americans, saw Senator Obama as a liberator of our nation from questionable policies, legislation, and indeed, wars that were initiated during the previous administration of President George W. Bush. His liberating, universal message of hope had earned him the Nobel Peace Prize in 2009.

We complement the act of remembering stories by acting on them. Often, you can remember your past, but it takes a different type of person to remember, and then act accordingly. I was counseling a parishioner, Rebecca, following her husband's death. Rebecca and Martin had been married for thirty years. A year had passed since his death, yet her grief was overwhelming. She was stuck in the mourning process and over-ritualizing her visits to the cemetery a few times per week. When she began telling me about her mother and son's deaths and how she coped with them, it dawned on me that she, indeed, had memories that could help her in this instance. I asked her to recall how she'd gotten through the earlier episodes of grief. Almost instantly, she remarked, "I see where you are going now!" Her countenance changed and I could feel the weight, lifting off her back.

This capacity for remembering lessons from the past distinguishes faith exemplars from those who are still growing their faith. It is reasonable to imagine that Dante and Debra, the congregants I observed who rededicated their lives, may have forgotten the spiritual lessons they've learned. Had they recalled their previous trials and experiences with the vicissitudes of life, and were able to summon those memories, they may have been able to calm their doubts or fears, knowing that a pearl of transformative and guiding wisdom abided with them. In this way, they could remain steadfast on their paths. In all likelihood, they had not completely forgotten the source of their faith, but such memories seemed to have receded into the background, becoming dormant. All of us have this experience from time to time. Intentionally growing our faith helps keep those lifelines at the forefront of our memory, so we're more likely to reach for them during times of need.

As of the writing of this book, Dante was still a member of the church where we had congregated. He continued being involved in various ministries, including music and ushering. Following his rededication, he could have been helped under spiritual direction or mentoring, partnering with someone who was sustained and mature in faith. But that congregation, like most, relied primarily on prayer. People pray for you, then you are sent back into the congregation on your own, with the faith that prayers will turn things around with the help of God.

Debra eventually joined a church of another denomination, similar to her previous theological orientation, and continued to be active in her church. Then something surprising happened. She began to draw upon her faith practices from African spirituality, including her Yoruba traditions. She reestablished important friendships, both church-related and otherwise. These seemed to provide her with a steadier footing on her faith journey, helping her cope better with life's trials and tribulations without feeling the need to start over when she encountered various bumps along the way.

Getting a hold of our faith does not mean we will no longer experience the trials and vicissitudes of life. Instead, we have memories that help us recall how we made it through the storms of life. It is not a matter of faith protecting you from difficulties.

Rather, faithing is a matter of knowing the presence of God and supportive people while undergoing difficulties.

Trusting the Experience of Others

Faithing is largely a communal experience. We are borne on the shoulders of those who have gone before us. The ability to trust the wisdom and experience of others is an essential trait for people who want to grow through a life of faith. The key to a rich life of faith is accepting the wisdom of others. That is, trusting what other people offer you as counsel and words to live by. You can often see the fruit of their faith in various ways, as they live their lives with love for others, generously and compassionately. In most faith communities, people will point out the faith leaders, and they make themselves known by looking out for the well-being and spiritual welfare of others. These are characteristics that are hard to fake.

In the Buddhist tradition, such a person might be called a bodhisattva. This is a person who has attained prajna, or enlightenment, but who postpones nirvana to help others to attain enlightenment: individual bodhisattvas are the subjects of devotion in certain sects and are often represented in painting and sculpture.

This is exactly how I decided to attend seminary following my career in finance. In a career transition outplacement course, the facilitator suggested that I consider a new career—the ministry. He thought I had the natural inquisitiveness and temperament for pastoral ministry. In my heart of hearts, I knew that his recommendation made perfect sense. I had inquired about religious studies a few years earlier. A week or so later, I was enrolled in my first Master of Divinity course at Perkins School of Theology.

When taking solicited or unsolicited advice of a spiritual nature, it is natural to want to check it out, reflect upon it, and perhaps discuss the matter with someone else. Many people will reject spiritual counsel outright, choosing to rely upon their own knowledge and experience. This can become problematic for those seeking more depth and breadth in their faith development because growing our faith is a process that works best in community, just as we all rely on others for support and growth in other areas of our lives.

Evolving, remembering, and trusting others: each of these qualities is important, and there is room for more. But for now, they are enough for us to lay out the components of faithing in the following chapters.

SECTION II

FROM FAITH TO EXEMPLARY FAITH

Chapter 3

How your story takes root and faith emerges

Faith arises from within us. Though we are influenced from the outside—by external experience—the seed of growth begins internally. Our thoughts, feelings, knowledge, beliefs, and memories are the basis for how we perceive who we are as human beings. Unless you are called by the universe to be a spiritual prophet at an early age, like the Buddha or Jesus, it is likely that it will take time for your faith to germinate and take root. But it is important to remember that it does take root. As you become more and more in touch with your personal story and begin seeing it as a source of faith that you can trust, your faith will grow deeper, sturdier roots.

I tend to trace my faith story back to my early adolescent years. One of my father's close friends had given me a copy of Kahlil Gibran's *The Prophet*. He knew I loved reading and must have seen a spark in my eye and my soul. I began devouring the book. At many places in the text, I felt a deep sense of resonance with the words, knowing immediately that they were true and wise. These seemed to validate my sense of the world, becoming a wiser person. As I read Gibran's words, they became a part of my story, re-instilling confidence that I was on the right path spiritually, and could keep doing what I was doing and be okay in the world.

This kind of experience is available to all of us. We need only to open ourselves to the possibility of experiences and noticing opportunities as they arise. Another way to say this is to imagine that every experience could have some meaning for us. This is not the same as "everything happens for a reason." What I'm saying is that reflecting on your experience intentionally enables you to discover meaning. This may not be "the" meaning, only a good enough meaning to move you along on your inward journey of faith.

Faith Produces "Fruit of the Spirit"

The internal sense of self that I developed as a youth is what I call "the fruit of the spirit."[2] If you imagine the spiritual or faith life as a tree with many branches, the fruits are what make up your faith story. All the elements that I mentioned earlier—thoughts, feelings, knowledge, beliefs, memories—are there. The tree produces many fruits. The quantity and quality depend on how faithfully you nurture the tree. In addition to these internal processes and experiences are behaviors, spiritual practices, relationships, vocational life, physical health, and so on. Each of these needs nurturing to grow. It is difficult to nurture all of these one hundred percent of the time. But with enough practice, over time, this can become second nature.

One of my spiritual mentors (by proxy) is Dave Ramsey, the financial guru. Dave specializes in helping people develop better money-management skills, but along the way, he discusses

---

[2] The term is not original. It comes from the Book of Galatians in the Bible: verses 5.22-23. Paul declares the fruit of the Spirit to be "love, joy, peace, patience, kindness, generosity, faithfulness, gentleness, and self-control." I have added growth in faith as one of the fruit, also.

relationship-building and smart business practices. He encourages his followers to become charitable as they become debt-free, developing generosity as they give. Putting it another way, we give in order to become generous people. The quality of being generous is a fruit of the spirit. It is a way of being in the world that demonstrates one's charitable heart, compassion for others, selflessness, and desire to make the world a better place. True generosity happens without expectations of getting something in return. Moreover, generosity is a way of living out the universal call of sharing ourselves (time, talents, and treasure) with others. Primarily, I am referring to financial generosity here. So, it is with other parts of the life in faith. If you practice what you want to become, it helps you become that person.

There are many other fruits of the spirit. These include love, joy, peace, patience, kindness, generosity, faithfulness, gentleness, and self-control.

You need not be an outwardly religious person to enjoy these gifts. Most of us learn about these virtues in our family and community. Even so, many seek out places of worship for more formal training and religious education on these aspects of living, especially when there are children in the family. For me, this highlights how powerful and important these elements of faith life are, the need to incorporate them into your self-concept. It is necessary to take them seriously. And when you notice them in others, try to point them out and raise the other person's awareness.

It is significant to identify which fruits of the spirit are yours. You can use the list provided earlier or you can develop your own list by paying attention to your heart and soul, responding accordingly. You may find that you do possess the gift of love. Loving yourself and discovering the sacred in daily living may come naturally to you. For some, love seems to flow out to the world effortlessly. For others, not so much. Instead, you may be gifted with patience. Others are naturally drawn to nature and find beauty in the earth. You may have a heightened sensitivity to issues of justice and fairness. All fruits of the spirit deserve to be nurtured and grown so that they can reproduce in the world. Ultimately, that is the purpose: to use your gifts to bring about a better world.

Here's a true story. I'm a fairly patient person. It takes quite a bit of drama to get my blood pressure up. But I wasn't born this way. I learned it gradually, over time, by nurturing a trait I had witnessed in a good friend named Otis. He was one of my fraternity brothers who was on an even keel, not overly excitable. One day, a group of us were running late to catch a flight out of Washington, D.C. Leaving our hotel downtown, we ran straight into a traffic jam. I panicked, telling the taxi driver which way to go—I was the worst kind of backseat driver! The more I stressed the steadier Otis remained. He didn't raise his voice, become anxious, or appear ruffled in any way. His inner calm and infinite patience astonished me. He helped me realize how irrational I was. I soon concluded that I needed some of what Otis had.

I started practicing patience immediately after that taxi ride. For me, that meant slowing down—learning to calm myself in real-time. I could no longer expect everything to happen rapidly on my terms, the way I wanted it, with little regard for others' needs and differences. Another way of practicing patience was to realize that hurrying was a self-induced perspective that I had no right to force upon others. And frequently my sense of immediacy was about things that could wait without serious consequences. It wasn't the easiest thing that I've ever done, but perhaps one of the best. Over time, it became easier and easier for me to practice patience because I had such an outstanding role model and memory of Otis during that storm. When I say, "Over time," I don't mean days or weeks, I mean months or years.

I found many opportunities to practice patience. Something as simple as standing in line at the grocery store and getting stuck in the slow line became a chance to slow down, practice my discipline, and develop patience. People began telling me, "You seem so patient!" I would smile and say, "Thank you," and have a conversation with that person. Its given me confidence as I've developed a new fruit of the spirit.

We all have fruits of the spirit within us—some more easily developed than others. Work with what you have and find opportunities to expand your gifts. Should you find these fruits difficult, there's no need to stress. We're not striving to be a Jack or of all trades; only to master the faith we choose and allow this to bear the fruit that it will.

How a Growing Faith Builds Confidence

An important by-product, or offshoot, of getting a hold of your faith is confidence in oneself, others, and the spirit of life. As with all other aspects of life, we master certain qualities when practicing consistently and with repetition. Over time, we become experts, or exemplars. If you are a software programmer and begin honing your craft as a teenager, by the time you are an adult, you may have grown from an apprentice to a mid-level journeyperson. If, while your peers are outside playing, and you are parked in front of a computer screen, it's highly likely by the time you reach the workforce you'll have a much greater advantage over your peers. By the time you reach young adulthood, you may be on the cusp of starting your own company. Your confidence in yourself and your abilities are boundless. The life of faith is exactly the same. The earlier you begin and the more you practice, whether by studying sacred texts from a culture of your choice, attending spiritual and religious services, and being around faith-minded people, your self-confidence on matters of faith can render a significant impact.

Chapter 4

Confidence leads to self-trust and creativity

It's important to continue growing and learning in a life of faith. Being open to life's challenges and opportunities expands your self-awareness, a vital aspect of maintaining strong faith. It's important to remain open to how the spirit of life may call you from different directions. Just as the winds of nature blow to the North and at other times, to the East. Be like a kite on a string and let the spirit take you. Having strong faith is about being open, not only to your calling in the world, but to the callings of others. The more relationships secured with people from other faith traditions and practices, the more your faith will be nurtured and grown.

As your faith takes flight, you will notice that your confidence spreads to other areas of life. It's no surprise. What you do habitually, you will eventually do instinctively. What you do well, in time, becomes second nature.

Though confidence arises from practicing faith, there is no right or wrong way to take hold of your faith. Yet, traditional religion may have us believe otherwise. Many will admonish you to attend worship services once or twice a week and may lay a guilt trip on you if you don't. Some insist upon diligent bible study and reading daily devotionals. Many churches and synagogues have a "path" or process for becoming immersed in the life of the congregation. I believe all of these are excellent approaches to grow in the life of faith. Yet, when it comes right down to it, we'd be more honest by admitting that we're making it up as we go along. This notion appeals to me because it leaves room for error, detours, and discovery. These aspects of faith development coincide with exemplary faith and the confidence to live one's life with integrity and boldness.

There are many resources to call upon as we fashion our journey of faith. The most important one is modeling other people of strong faith. Try to replicate their ways of living out their faith convictions. When you find someone whom you consider an exemplar of faith, ask that person for a discussion about *their* path. People love talking about their faith journey!

When I was in seminary, I recall an assignment in my spiritual direction course where everyone interviewed someone fundamental to their faith life. I thought I was being clever by selecting my mother for my first interview. She, indeed, surprised me with her faith story. But it turned out that almost everyone in the class did the same thing—interviewed a parent. We cannot always query our parents. They may be deceased, incapacitated, or even estranged from you. If your parents are not available, I encourage you to find another faith elder to interview and adopt their ethical values. Similarly, if you don't consider your parents to be exemplary, or perhaps they're not involved in your choice of faith practices, you can find someone else in your family whom you consider wise, trustworthy, and living an exemplary life.

Another way on your journey is to join a community of forward-thinking exemplars. These are people who see the world as sunny side up. You can hardly get enough of these people in your life because they help transform your ability to conceive what is possible. Nothing beats a can-do attitude for growth. This sounds like common sense, but I'm continually surprised by the abundance of complainers in the world and the scarcity of those who shine. You have to keep your eyes open for people who are beacons of light and allow yourself to walk in their direction. Since we tend to gravitate toward like-minded people, if you want serious change, you have to be deliberate when seeking out those who create change with the future in mind.

Faith practices are the other critical resource. Traditional religion has a head start, as sacred texts tend to lay out how historical religious figures carved out their spiritual paths, and we have copied their examples down through the years. But humanist and other non-traditional spiritualities are equally ripe for spiritual practice. It means we need to be creative and use all the resources around us. Or, we can make them up. The book *Everyday Spiritual Practice*, edited by a Unitarian Universalist minister, Scott Alexander, is a wonderful place to discover how to make the ordinary sacred. I appreciate this book because it shows a variety of writers describing spiritual practice in everyday life. This book encourages you to examine your actions as a pathway for experiencing the divine.

There is a chapter in the book *A Spiritual Maintenance Schedule*, by the Rev. Arvid Straube, which emphasizes the need for a daily, weekly, and yearly spiritual practice. That means doing something every day, something on a weekly schedule (preferably spending time in a group), and incorporating an annual pilgrimage or retreat into your routine. My point is that Straube is saying, "There are hundreds of practices and techniques available to you, if only you are creative and "help your heart find its way on the path." The aim is to make all of your life a spiritual practice.

One of my parishioners, Sharon, a classical music lover and a mindfulness practitioner developed a way of bringing her two passions together, which opened up her spiritual life. When she drives through scenic areas of her town, she plays classical music on the radio. As the music plays, she intentionally seeks to "get inside" the music by imagining she is there with the musicians watching their every move and sensing the conductor as he brings out the best of every player. As Sharon focuses on the music, she tries to keep other thoughts from entering her meditation. When other thoughts creep in, she notices them and returns to the music. She engages in this practice once or twice a day, or as often as her driving allows. Over time, she has not only turned listening to classical music into a spiritual practice, she has also boosted her ability to concentrate in unexpected ways. Her practice is as innovative as the walking meditation of Thich Nhat Hanh.

I love this type of creativity regarding spiritual practice! Sharon is the perfect example of how to find opportunities for spiritual growth when in a routine, or even during mundane daily activities. There is no limit to the number of ways we can incorporate spirituality into our lives. I recently read how citizens around the globe have been feeding birds and other wildlife in their yards and gardens as a means of engaging with nature. This has been going on in the last century. Many people who maintain bird feeders feel they are helping the birds make it through the winter. I view this practice as having spiritual potential because the underlying principle is that humans have a duty to respect the life of all living creatures. Many indigenous religions and spiritual groups live out this same principle. Native American religion is one of those. In Native American culture, we are considered part of the earth and all of nature, enhanced by meaningful ceremonies and symbols. We can make this an intentional spiritual practice by bringing our awareness to it, as Sharon did with her music and mindfulness practice.

Research on Americans' desire for balance in their lives by the noted scholar Daniel Kahneman suggests that people want more spirituality in their daily routines, especially women. While spiritual practice is perceived as adding significant balance and quality to our lives, according to the American Time Use Survey in 2014, we devote more time to television by a ratio of 20:1. This degree of misalignment brings fewer pleasures and growth, defeating the practices needed to enhance our spiritual lives. I strongly encourage you to make a mental note of this, then go a step further by actually incorporating spiritual practice into your daily life experiences. Make it a reality, not just a dream.

The more we learn to view our creativity as a vital part of our life's work, the more we develop confidence in ourselves. By understanding creativity and confidence as an integral part of spiritual life, we open up our whole lives to being an act of faith. Or as the Rev. Arvid Straube beckons us, we can make our whole lives a spiritual practice.

Chapter 5

The Faith of Our Ancestors and Role Models

As a pastoral counselor, I've met people who have spent much of their lives trying to avoid being like their parents. Many have good reasons for that. With faith, however, we are often better off using our ancestors as role models. Those who struggled to survive and were able to thrive are particularly good candidates to use as exemplars. Using the metaphor from the Apostle Paul, we are "grafted" onto the faith lives of those who went before us.

Speaking of Paul, his life's work was calling the people of the ancient world to a new life of faith. He was a former Jew who saw Jesus' ministry as an outgrowth of the Jewish tradition. Although, truth be told, altogether different. *Grafting* refers to tying a broken branch onto a living tree to keep it growing. This metaphor is apt for an exemplary faith journey. Those of us with ancestors strong in faith and essence, tend to outgrow an existing faith. By listening to their faith stories and how they grew in faith over time, we activate within us a source of faith that is ready to come alive.

Parents, Grandparents, and Others Transmit Faith to Future Generations

For many of us, our parents and grandparents became great sources of inspiration. If you're like me, most of these people have passed on, and perhaps, you were never able to meet them. In that case, you'll want to seek out similar figures for conversations. With such beloved people, we can look back together upon their lives and see the struggles overcome, disappointments assuaged, and hard work turned into success. If we look deep enough and listen carefully, we will hear the same type of narratives concerning their faith. The narratives are there for the taking. We only need to fine-tune our listening.

This is especially important when we consider our definition of faithing.

Faithing is maintaining an awareness of the transcendent presence. By leaning on our ancestors—parents, grandparents, and other spiritual exemplars—and their stories of transcendence, we can be grafted onto this same awareness. What they did, we can do. Being aware of this inheritance of faith makes it real and visible in our own lives.

When we think about people who search their genealogy by consulting historical documents, what comes to mind is someone tracing their family tree to its roots. They want to know where they came from. Who were their ancestors? At some point in their search, if they are lucky, they'll meet someone with stories about their grandparents and great-grandparents, uncles and aunts, and so on. From these lively stories, we gain a better sense of who we are, or, as we often say, *whose* are we.[3] This same trek through

---

3   "Whose are we" refers to our sense of belonging and tends to suggest a special emphasis on our faith community. As infants, we belong to our parents or other caregivers. And as we age, our sense of belonging evolves when we join and leave

the family genealogy can be, and should be, applied to our faith journey since it can help us grow into ourselves in a meaningful way. By actively seeking out these stories from our parents, parents' siblings, grandparents, elder friends and family, we can take an active role in developing our faith.

I cherish a story passed down to me from my father, an avowed atheist, yet a person of deep (non-religious) faith. He shared the story of how his father, (my grandfather, whom I'd never met) was a deacon in the Baptist Church that was one block up the street and over the hill from where I grew up. My mother still lives there. My grandfather was a founding deacon of the church, and his name, along with the other founding deacons, is engraved on the cornerstone. As a deacon, his role was to help the pastor take care of members in various ways, such as delivering food to people who were sick or home bound. My father did not consider his father to be *religious* in the traditional sense of the word. But he did see him as being faithful to the church through his service to the people of the community. Watching my father's life unfold, I learned about two similar dispositions of my father and my grandfather. He'd often help people in the neighborhood and the larger community. It is clear to me that I have been grafted onto this tradition as well, although I *am* a declared person of faith and a minister. The same might be true for you as well. You only need to seek out the stories of faith that lies within your family tree.

---

groups and communities. Persons on the spiritual path also want to live out their need to belong to a community of meaning; one that confirms our need to associate with goodness, and to contribute to the greater good. People of faith, both religious and secular, sense that something bigger than themselves has a claim on their lives. That stirs up in them a drive to aspire and dream. We might say that that a larger force informs us about "whose" are we.

Role Models Demonstrate Strong Faith Through Convictions, Practices, and Actions

My example is open to all who seek opportunities that are within arm's reach—a phone call, email, or conversation over a cup of coffee. If your family has no faith history, you are not precluded from this journey. But you will have to take a different type of approach. It will involve immersing yourself in a faith community of your choosing and seeking out people you look up to and befriend intentionally. Ask questions and pick their brains about how they chose their path. Every faith tradition, whether Unitarian Universalism, Buddhism, Judaism, or humanism, has its exemplars who are just waiting to tell their story. They will enjoy teaching others about convictions and practices that made them who they are. This is not to suggest that these people are easy to find, they often are not. But they are out there lying in wait for those ready to grow and get a hold of their faith.

Many are inspired by the life of the Buddha, who by any measure was an example of faith. Tradition holds that Siddhartha Gautama was born into wealth, and his parents raised him to lead a life fit for a prince. He, like many present-day pilgrims, was brought up in one religious tradition, thought to be Vedic Brahmanism, and not exposed to other faiths. His father was determined Siddhartha be protected from the suffering in the world. Siddhartha lived for twenty-nine years royally yet sensing that something prevailed beyond his protected world. When he finally left the royal palace to meet his people, he quickly came in contact with the sick, aged, and suffering. But it was the encounter with an old man that removed the scales from his eyes. For the first time, he learned that everyone ages. Later, he met a diseased man, a decaying corpse, and a person living as an ascetic in an austere and abstinent spiritual life. These encounters with reality beyond the palace walls inspired Siddhartha to pursue the life of an ascetic himself.

Over the centuries, many have found the Buddha's story of transformation to be the epitome of a spiritual journey worthy of duplication. It is a remarkable story.

Rather than trying to duplicate Siddhartha's journey, I encourage you to find your path of spiritual redemption or transformation. That is, if you choose the Buddhist path, allow it to take you where it will. You are, of course, free to renounce your wealth and privilege if so-called, but know that it is not necessary to mimic the Buddha's path to find the truth. What you may take from the tradition is his sincere determination to answer a call that arose from within him and allow that pursuit to unravel naturally. If the ascetic life calls you and you feel that path is *the* authentic way, follow it. This enables you to use the Buddha as an example of exemplary faith while maintaining the necessary freedom to develop *your* faithing process.

Another possibility that is open to all is to find an example of exemplary faith through various forms of media. Whether through sacred literature, novels, self-help manuals, films, poetry, or YouTube, it can be done. The beauty of this approach is accessibility. In the digital age, there's a wealth of materials at our fingertips. Anyone with access to a laptop, tablet, computer, smartphone, or library card, for that matter, can discover and follow the faith example of their choosing. Eventually, it will become necessary to take your newly grafted-on faith into the real world where you interact with people. There you can practice and activate your faith, test out your convictions, and let them grow. This is the only way that faith grows and matures.

A Word of Caution Regarding Abusive Relationships

An important caveat is necessary here. For persons who have a tainted or abusive faith history—especially if persons of trust were involved—the metaphor of being "grafted on" is not appropriate. Getting far away from this history or the perpetrators might be a necessary intervention. Professionally speaking, I would encourage people with troubled personal histories to associate with trusted religious or spiritual figures, to seek a trained mental health professional, or a spiritual director who is competent in healing this type of psychic and emotional pain. A professional who is sensitive to this need can help the healing begin so the path to exemplary faith can be re-established healthily.

Chapter 6

Faith Threads

Back in the seventies, hipsters used to refer to clothes as "threads." You'd see a guy you knew at a party and you'd say, "Man, those are some nice threads you're wearing!" It was a huge compliment and using the word "threads" made you feel cool. The word "thread" also refers to an *idea* that runs through a story. This meaning makes threads directly applicable to finding your faith, which is often a result of a person's life story. A *faith thread* is a unifying theme or meaning that runs through a person's faith story. And just as a garment is made of many threads stitched together, many faith threads form the garment of your life—which, when reflected upon intentionally—can help you envision yourself as a faith exemplar. The journey that I have in mind is reviewing your life for experiences of meeting challenges, realizing success, and maintaining resilience.

Learning How to Reflect by Observing Others

Some people have a knack for learning from reflection. They can have an experience, naturally reflect upon that experience, and systematically find lessons to put into action to generate better results for their future. This is a gift from the universe, or perhaps, inherited from one's parents. For others, reflection is a practice that can be learned, which can pay big dividends by finding threads of faith. Once you discover the faith threads of your life, you will automatically begin to put them into a meaningful tapestry that helps you make sense of your life and who you are.

Hospital chaplaincy programs are excellent for teaching chaplain residents (similar to physician residents). Their methodology is called the "action, reflection, action" method. It works like this: chaplains have an encounter with a patient, staff member, or family. Then they write up a report form and present it to a group of other chaplain residents and the supervisor. The "chaplain residents" in conjunction with the chaplain supervisor, helps these chaplains reflect on what happened to find some meaning and lessons from the experience. (Importantly, there is no right or wrong answer.) Then the chaplain takes that group experience and turns it into a part of their faith development. Over time, each chaplain learns to do this on their own.

One of the most important lessons I learned from this training was that the supervisors had a way of highlighting the most positive aspects of the experience, which reinforced each chaplain's confidence, sense of authority, and identity as a minister. Indeed, I came to this conclusion by reflecting on my own learning experience. It happened when I realized I was doing a lot of interesting forms of ministry right during my tenure as a chaplain resident. I was learning and growing a lot in terms of ministerial identity.

Yet, after reflecting on this change over time, it dawned on me that it was the *supervisors* that were doing things differently, to my benefit. They had a way of both supporting and leading me to experience myself differently than I would if I had been practicing alone. In essence, by doing ministry, reflecting on what

I'd done, then doing more of the same with minor tweaks, I was slowly changing and emerging into someone new.

You might ask, how did I put this learning to use? The answer is quite simple. I began copying my chaplain supervisors' techniques! As you'll see later, I flipped the script and became a cheerleader for others! I've realized that almost all people benefit from positive feedback.

Noticing what people do right and speaking feedback directly back to them helps develop faith in themselves. I use this with almost everyone I come in contact with. That includes my work as a minister supervising my staff, as a military chaplain with chaplain assistants, with people I meet in passing, my friends and especially with my wife. With constant practice, reflecting in a positive way on what I see around me has become second nature. Even during ordinary conversations at the gym, I can practice this type of reflection with people. This way of being is part of my faith thread, or more specifically, my faith identity. I see myself as a "faith promoter" of sorts.

Listening for Faith Threads in Stories

You don't have to be a chaplain or chaplain resident to benefit from this excellent form of learning. Nor do you need a chaplain supervisor. It is possible to acquire this skill by watching those you encounter who tell their stories well. You will find by observing them that there is usually a thread, or theme, that runs through their stories and remembrances. Truthfully, the best people who do this have an excellent memory and a natural ability to spin a tale. Or they've read enough to be able to incorporate bits and pieces of stories into their own. Whatever the situation, the thread is the part that resonates from within the person. It adheres, and over time becomes a part of their ongoing faith narrative. Being a student of people helps with this strategy because it opens you up to different ways of living out your faith narrative.

I've had a pastoral counseling client who came for several sessions to discuss his recurring bouts of depression. After several sessions, it became clear that the depression was a symptom of his lack of purpose. During each visit, he began telling stories of his former work life. He'd been a stockbroker in a previous career, which provided him a lot of fulfillment. He talked about helping former clients build up their portfolios and he sensed their gratitude for teaching them to understand the stock market. As it turned out, it wasn't the results his clients had, but the gratification he gained by sharing himself with others that he remembered so fondly. His thread of teaching gradually emerged. When teaching others a new skill, he'd come alive. This insight helped him cope more effectively with his depression by recognizing that he was his best self when helping others.

Pick Up Your Mentors Along the Way

Another way of discovering your faith threads is to enlist a person you enjoy talking to who will naturally draw out your own story. All of us love certain people because we feel so at home with them, and we're able to be our most genuine selves in their presence. We usually call them our best friend forever, BFF, or so-called *bestie*. Other people may have chemistry with you, which elicits more sharing of yourself with some people than you'd naturally share with others. The person who has this ability to help you deepen your reflections is the one you'd be searching for.

If you can find a person who does this concerning spiritual matters or issues of faith, this person may become your spiritual mentor. They won't even have to know it. The relationship need not be formalized to work. Your person only needs to elicit a mental-spiritual response from you that helps you ground your inner life more deeply. Find ways to spend time with such people like this, and, as you do, listen to yourself telling your own story. Discover what rises to the surface of your narrative that has been important to your faith development. This will be your faith thread.

Reflect, Summarize, Learn From Your Mistakes and Regroup

Developing this capacity for reflection helps you when something happens in your life that necessitates a review of your past. Having the ability to occasionally look back, summarize, learn what went right or wrong, then regroup, lends itself to tapping into our faith threads, and therefore, developing deeper faith. I use the word *capacity* because it recalls our internal power or ability, natural or learned, to get something done. The human tendency is to look back searching for what went wrong, beat ourselves up over it, then believe that the whipping will help us become better. Research shows improvement usually doesn't work this way. In fact, the more we focus on the positive and the more *compassionate* we are to ourselves when things don't go perfectly (which they rarely do), the greater chance we'll have of building more capacity for improvement.

Faith threads transform into exemplary faith by highlighting and repurposing stories already within us. Experiences that make us who we are have different meanings throughout our lives.

What was unimportant in our twenties can be monumentally important to us in our forties, once we've learned how to look back with faith in mind. The faith and courage referenced in our younger selves can help us be bold, creative, and courageous in our later years by sharing these stories. If we can find that trusted friend or enlist a faith mentor to help us uncover these vital experiences, the chances are great that faith will come.

Here is an example. Part of my childhood experience revolved around living in a mixed socioeconomic neighborhood. I learned from my parents, people at church, and school the necessity of helping those in need. One day, one of my good friends at school was teased by other kids because he was wearing worn-out shoes. I recall feeling sad for him, and wanted to speak up, but felt powerless to interfere. I was just a skinny kid, I told myself. For many years, I felt remorse for not opening my mouth on his behalf. He did a pretty good job of it himself, but still, the regret lingered on. The primary theme in that story was justice and fairness. To this day, I feel a deep resonance within me when I encounter injustices. What I've surmised from that earlier experience, that story, is that *justice* and *helping* are faith threads for me. When I read articles, headlines, or hear stories that involve justice and fairness issues, they naturally pique my interest, and sometimes, lead me to action. In this manner I am often reflecting and learning from my experiences, being vigilant about refining how I articulate my faith threads in service of justice and fairness.

The Evolution of Sustaining Faith

The capacity to grow in faith is an evolutionary process that continues throughout our lives. Wherever you begin is a fine place to start. But once you do begin, don't waste your time. Start reflecting on your past and present experiences. Search your memory for threads of faith that string together "who you are." Look for common themes and allow them to emerge through conversation with people you admire and those who admire you. Eventually, you will find yourself coming into your faith. Never stop, keep evolving!

Chapter 7

Executing Your Faith

One of the greatest benefits of growing your faith is unlocking your life to invite the unknown, along with developing the capacity to embrace what you find through execution or by acting on your faith.

Being able to execute exemplary faith opens the door to possibilities.

This happens when we allow our confidence, trust, and ultimately our hope, to propel us toward "acting as if" what we hope for will unfold for us. This does not equate with shifting your life onto automatic pilot, or to what is known as "magical thinking," which tricks people into believing that thinking without action or effort leads to results. This is a common error for many people of faith. To clear this up once and for all, let us spend some time debunking some of the errors associated with "execution." Then, we will explore more life-affirming ways of understanding what it means to execute one's faith.

Myth #1: A Supreme Being Will Fix Our Lives

Executing our faith is not hoping that a supreme being will fix our lives. While I do not deny the existence of a supreme being, I do not believe that a supreme being structures our lives or sets a course for us. That is what human initiative and responsibility is about:

Passively waiting for miracles to happen, or even simple change, is self-defeating.

First, it takes you out of the game of life where change is a result of effort and action.

Second, it diminishes the personal power that you have within yourself to effect change.

Third, it robs you of your sense of responsibility for your life.

None of these are grounded in taking an active role in your future. The song by Billie Holiday comes to mind: "God Bless the Child That's Got His Own." The title implies that a transcendent power expects us to work with what we've been born with, given, or developed. We don't sit around doing nothing, hoping that good things will come our way.

Consider this example. The spiritual advisor and life coach Iyanla Vanzant specializes in helping individuals and families get their lives in order by working through difficult problems— some that have plagued them for years. She guides them through serious reflection by asking difficult, yet honest questions related to how their decisions and actions, and often lack of taking responsibility for their lives, have led to the crises that they find themselves in.

Vanzant writes about her transformation from such crises in her books. As a person of deep faith and one called to practice as a Yoruba healer, she learned through deep loss that her wisdom and discernment were required to get to the other side of pain to healing. After establishing a name for herself through her writings and motivational speaking, her faith was tested when her daughter was diagnosed with cancer. Relying on expensive alternative treatments and praying for natural healing, they found themselves on a downward spiral resulting in her daughter's death. Then Vanzant's marriage dissolved. Later came financial ruin. She realized that she had to turn inward to her resources to climb out of a terrible chain of events. She reported that she had to face truths about her belief system and life philosophy that no longer worked. No supreme being alone could fix things. She had to rely on herself.

It is hard work. Often, the individual and families she coaches spiritually uncover deep-seated pain, and as they work through the root causes of their crises, many cry, scream at each other, and verbally spar. But eventually, they realize they have the resources needed to fix their lives.

Growing our faith is a similar process. Getting a hold of your life won't happen on its own. You must be deliberate, conscious, and willing to put in the effort. It is hard work. Fortunately, the dividends are enormous and worth every ounce of toil.

Myth #2: Believing Does Not Equal Executing

By the same token, executing your faith is not the same as belief, or maintaining a set of beliefs. We learn this unequivocally from the religion professor James Carse, author of *The Religious Case Against Belief,* who associates belief with having the certainty that one's convictions are true, but not being amenable to correct those convictions if necessary. Another type of impediment is the use of various forms of empirical testing, which can be hypothetical or unsubstantiated. Using the example of Martin Luther when he confronted the Holy Roman Emperor, Carse characterizes beliefs and belief systems as:

Large intellectual schemes [that] often have distinctive historical narratives, extensive mythology, a pronounced sense of community, a pantheon of heroes and martyrs, an array of symbols, scripted rituals, sacred geographical sites and monuments, [and] on top of all of this is an absolute certainty in the truth of their beliefs.

This description of belief reveals its inward and provincial nature. It has more to do with mental structures and closing off the individual and community while keeping the notion of God, or a supreme being, and being sequestered from others. Activating faith, on the other hand, is about action and openness to possibility *beyond* your current knowledge. It also commends us to the wisdom of others and the freedom and relationships found within and beyond our community.

You will still maintain beliefs that are important and foundational to your faith. You will also maintain your knowledge base and continue striving to build upon it. Knowledge contributes to belief. Moreover, you will continue holding on to your religious and spiritual convictions, and although growing faith may encourage you to challenge them, you can apply more rigor. Religious convictions and beliefs strengthen faith, too. Those beliefs should not be equated with faith, however. Faith goes beyond that which we claim to already know.

Execution Means Creating a Plan of Action

Executing faith is about creating a plan of action and sticking to it. The most direct route to achieving execution is by choosing a spiritual practice, committing yourself to a schedule and making it a part of your routine. But for those who are less apt to jump right in, developing a plan of attack is another surefire way of living out one's faith commitments. I like the metaphor "plan of attack" because it connotes a concerted effort to get something done. It also suggests that we are getting rid of something that stands in our way. In this case, it is inaction or lack of faith commitments, faith threads, or any other form of inertia.

A plan might consist of spending certain minutes a day in meditation or private study to ground your spiritual practice. It may consist of setting your intention, similar to the Buddhist practice, at the start of the new day to put the practice into motion. There are countless ways to plan your faith development. But most central to this plan is recording it, writing it down, and making it physically visible to you during the day, as a real and constant reminder of the promise you've made to yourself to make a concerted effort to get this done. You can pin your plan to your refrigerator or bulletin board you look at daily, create a note on your computer, write in your *moleskin*, or make a smartphone reminder. Anything that you have to look at frequently will serve the purpose adequately.

The plan might also include where you will do your spiritual practices, how frequently, and most important, signs (observations) to look for that your spiritual disciplines are producing fruit. Sometimes, the signs are subjective and intangible. For example, as a result of practicing yoga, you may feel more gratitude toward life and become aware of more joy in your heart due to your commitment to practice consistently. After your yoga practice, you can feel your body growing more supple and limber as your ability to stretch develops with difficult poses. The more you can add such details, the greater probability that you'll stick to your plan. Sometimes:

the more incremental the detail

the easier it will be to begin the task

and the more likely you'll do it.

In pastoral counseling, we often ask a client, "What is the smallest step you can take toward your new goal?" Here, the smallest thing is often the easiest, and therefore, more likely to get done. Continuing with the yoga example, the smallest step may be scheduling the yoga class on your calendar, then set aside the time so that no distractions derail you. If you're more advanced in your routine, perhaps place your yoga mat in your car, or in the front seat where you see it. This could be the smallest thing. The idea is to do something small yet significant that prompts you to act in the way you know is best for your spiritual practice.

I love to exercise, and over the years, it's become a part of my lifestyle. I was in Lima, Peru on vacation and found a gym for exercising daily within two days of my arrival. Many people don't have this level of drive and the stick-to-it mentality, so they need more assistance or motivators. A recent trend is the use of personal devices that monitor one's steps and transmit the data to a computer or a smartphone. Strapping on the device is a physical reminder of one's commitment to exercise, and a motivator to execute the exercise regimen. Executing your faith is similar. We need reminders, physical and mental, of our commitment to live faithfully, according to our convictions.

On many days, I use the *Illuminations* app on my smartphone. The app, developed by the Unitarian Universalist Association, puts "inspirational words" right at your fingertips. It opens automatically in the morning and reminds me to stop for a few moments to contemplate the sacredness of life. On your smartphone, you can do a simple Google search and download it. If you are not a smartphone user, it can be found on the Unitarian Universalist Association (UUA) website, http://www.uua.org/beliefs/illuminations. Much of the material on *Illuminations* is available on the UUA Worship Web, another outstanding source of faith-affirming readings, prayers, and meditations. If you choose Worship Web, you'll find the materials categorized differently, of course, but you can find them by searching.

My wife's close friend sends her a daily scripture along with a meditation. Whatever method you choose, execute it frequently enough and it will become a part of your lifestyle.

These practices remain ongoing throughout your life, or until you feel you have outgrown their usefulness. At that time, I encourage you to find something new to keep you stimulated and engaged in your inner life. It is quite possible that as you grow in exemplary faith, you may become a transmitter of faith—a person who actively and intentionally spreads the good news of your faith to others, which I consider to be a different expression than consuming faith materials for your edification. Even at this stage of the journey, it is important to maintain contact with sources of edifying and uplifting writings and teachings to maintain your grounding, reverence, and acknowledgment of the transcendent. I offer this primarily as a safeguard that we do not idolize ourselves.

When Execution is Difficult to Get Started

Taking the very first step is an important aspect of any plan. Let us take a lesson from the professionals. In a short-term and brief therapy practice, the therapist knows how hard it is for someone to execute new behaviors. Many clients struggle greatly to develop a plan. So, the therapist will often ask clients, "What is the smallest thing that you can do to get yourself started?" Counseling theory argues that smaller increments of action tend to generate more success. If you want to save money for a vacation, you don't try saving your whole paycheck because that leaves nothing to live off of. Instead, you put away a portion of every paycheck over a period of time. Let's say a year is a good goal. At the end of the year, you should have the targeted amount ready to pay for your trip. The same strategy applies when exercising faith. Small steps lead to big changes over time.

For example, a person who wants to begin the practice of journaling can easily be self-defeated by reasoning that having strong faith means mastering the task all at once. Mastery here might mean setting aside time to journal every day for perhaps five minutes and recording that day's experiences. On top of that, you can promise yourself to journal on Monday, Wednesday, and Friday. In actuality, it might take weeks or months of steady practice with one's journal to find a rhythm before the practice becomes a discipline. But instead of taxing yourself with big expectations, taking a few small steps at a time can help you solidify the practice until it becomes a satisfying spiritual exercise.

I mention journaling as an example of a spiritual discipline that has several payoffs in developing your faith. Each of these benefits, in my mind, is tangible, and not something you can just feel or sense is taking place. To begin with, journaling produces a cathartic effect. By recording your reflections and thoughts, you gather them up in a central place, with both in your psyche and on your document, so that they can be released into the care of the universe. This discipline then transforms into an important form of self-care as you learn to soothe yourself as no one else can. David Schnarch writes that "Being able to calm yourself down, soothe your hurts, and regulate your anxieties" is the mark of a balanced personality. Experiences that generate emotions such as anger, resentment, disgust, or hatred, can be captured in a journal in personal ways that need not be shared with the world. Writing them down also helps frame the emotions or examine the context in which they arise, if more action is required. Journaling is a means to accomplish this essential way of caring for yourself.

Journaling also helps build the habit of jotting down important ideas, observations, or intuitions before they escape your mind. Even those with the best memories need to jot down ideas before they evaporate. Your intuitions regarding your spiritual life, are equally worth capturing on paper, via a Word document, text messages to yourself, or a note file on your tablet. You may want to capture thoughts describing the beauty of a sunrise or a prayer resting on your heart. If you get in the habit of this practice, you'll discover that it reinforces your sense of self and develops a feeling of sturdiness that comes in handy when you need to rely on yourself for answers.

Nothing provides an audit trail of spiritual growth like a journal. You'll either look back on your old entries and remember when you were in that place or state of mind, or you won't remember writing it down at all, and wonder "Who was that person?" or "What does that even mean?" I believe that each of us is who we are due to hundreds of small decisions at different forks in the road, and dozens of more significant light bulb moments prompting us to tweak some part of our daily routine. A journal allows you to capture some of those encounters with the world that influences us to change our ways.

Probably the biggest advantage of the practice of spiritual journaling is that it gives you a definitive record of getting through difficult times. If written in a way to use as a reference, it might serve as a surefire reminder of how you have dealt with difficult times in the past. This can remind you of getting through the vicissitudes of life, again.

One parishioner used a creative method for journaling. He was a busy person and didn't have a lot of time at the end of the day for heavy journaling. Yet, he still knew the spiritual and therapeutic benefits of reflection and looking back on the day's events, as well as engaging in a meditative practice. So instead of writing full paragraphs, he would record certain words that stood out for him from the day. He might record big themes, such as gratitude, compassion, conversation, anger, tiredness, or "great day." This practice, though somewhat truncated from what one typically thinks about journaling, helped him solidify his experience, and most importantly, it helped him develop the discipline needed to reinforce his faith threads. Over time, his small steps could develop into bigger steps, or as the late astronaut, Neil Armstrong said, "A giant leap" of faith.

Incidentally, I later tried that parishioner's journaling method for my practice. I found it effective in helping me look back on my day and consider the highlights, and also derive some meaning from day-to-day. It seemed like an effective shortcut. A funny thing happened, however, when I returned to that journal months later and looked over those entries. I couldn't remember what any of the words meant! But I do know they worked during the time I wrote them.

Another parishioner visited me to discuss ways of coping with a medical condition that was progressively worsening. Accompanying his physical decline was a predisposition toward depression that had ran in his family. Fully aware of his tendency to adopt a self-defeating mindset, he wanted to develop positive habits that focused his attention on reasons to be grateful. He was already sending his partner a daily uplifting quote, but he needed something for himself. I suggested that he begin his day journaling about the goodness in his life. I sensed by his response to my suggestion that this had been a light bulb moment for him. Although his health was declining, he knew he had many blessings—among them, a son he was very proud of, a job that valued his contributions, and good health insurance. He said, "You are exactly right! I need to find ways to remind myself of these things, so I don't sabotage myself."

The next time I saw him, he expressed thanks for the visit and reported that his outlook was improving gradually. It is important to note that in cases like this, I also encourage parishioners to seek professional help—a licensed therapist, a physician, and even consider joining a support group—to get a handle on their mental health. Spiritual practices certainly contribute to wellness but are not a substitute for medical attention.

On the other hand, your spiritual practice may be going out in nature, going for a hike or bike ride, seeing yourself as an integral part of the leaves and trees of life.

This perhaps is the greatest learning for us about faith development: many small steps amalgamate, creating voluminous faith over time. The larger faith that we live out today cannot be dissected piece by piece.

As the pieces (conversations, readings of sacred and secular materials, ongoing practice, reflection, and countless forms of innovative faith work) coalesce inside of us, they are grafted on to who we are. Like a stream that flows into a river, it cannot be sifted out from the river. It all becomes one.

Chapter 8

Empowered to Live with Life's Mysteries

We spent years living in an age of perceived certainty. Between the information available at our fingertips via the internet and the so-called "twenty-four-hour news cycle," it is possible to deceive ourselves that we have answers to all of life's questions. Get sick. Go to the internet and *Google* the symptoms, and bam! the mystery of the illness has been solved. Want to know what the weather will be like when you arrive in San Francisco? Turn on the *Weather Channel* and get a five day forecast right away. Want an analysis of race relations in the United States after two terms of the first African American president with a liberal spin? *Salon.com* or the *Huffington Post* is waiting for you! None of this perceived certainty does a thing for growing our faith, though.

Unfortunately for us (or should I say, fortunately), some parts of the human experience remain cloaked in mystery. When tragedy or something unexpected occurs, such as a jet disappearing beyond the latest radar technology or someone whom we love dies, we are left with questions of why, how, and what? Why did it have to happen? How can I make it better for her or him? What will I do with myself now that I'm left behind?

There are unlimited amounts of similar questions, but they are not questions of faith. In many cases, there are no right or wrong answers. In fact, the more we ask "why" under such circumstances, the less we're able to confront the reality of what is left behind. We can become entrenched in the past and stuck in the mire of the false belief that it's necessary to know every why, how, and what. Better yet, we feel that we are *entitled* to know.

Mystery is Defined by the Unknown

"Knowing" might be said to be the opposite of mystery, and therefore, it is considered *unfaith*. Knowing more, that is, having more knowledge, does not grow one's faith. Instead, it may be counterproductive to exemplary faith.

Becoming a person of faith, then, is about living with unknowing. In other words, it is about living with mystery.

Merriam-Webster defines *mystery* as "a religious truth that one can know only by revelation and cannot fully understand." This definition fits perfectly with exemplary faith because those with strong faith are those who wait for life to be revealed. When they encounter something that is not immediately, or fully, understood, they can "roll with it."

You see, life is full of mystery. This is the chief reality of our existence.

They've grown to expect mystery and uncertainty and view it as an opportunity to live their faith. If you've ever walked alone down a dark street, you know that there's some uncertainty about what might be lurking in the veil of darkness. Yet, you trust your experience that it is safe to proceed. In the back of your mind, you hope that you can handle whatever might appear. You hope for the best.

Persons of exemplary faith relish the mystery of life instead of living with fear.

Another way to experience mystery is the trust fall. If you've been on a leadership retreat in the desert or a camping trip in the wilderness, guides will often build group cohesiveness or confidence by leading small groups of people using trust falls. A trust fall works in a couple of ways. The simplest form is asking one participant to stand behind another. The person in front gradually leans back until they fall, while the person in the rear stands firm and ready to catch them. No one hits the ground.

The more edgy version of the trust fall involves strapping a person into a harness, which is tied to a rope. The other team members stand at the opposite end of the rope holding the harnessed person. Then, the person stands facing away from the edge of a cliff or a steep drop-off. The people holding the rope (in tug-of-war style) gradually allow the harnessed person to lean back over the edge. Before the person gets into a perpendicular position, they're pulled back upright. In both cases, the person leaning has to trust that their companions will not let them fall off the cliff to the rocks below. Despite minimal chances that anyone will get hurt in the exercise, there remains just enough mystery to create some anxiety and doubt as to the person being caught by the others. "Should or can I do this?" is a common thought that pops into one's mind.

Some people cannot bring themselves to do this exercise. They are paralyzed by fear. I recall my own experience on a military confidence course. During my Commissioned Officer

Training, all students were put on a confidence course to test our mettle. There were about twenty obstacles involving jumping, running, climbing, hoisting oneself, and balancing. I tackled the course and had a great time. Then I returned to the course a year later during my Basic Chaplain Course. Most of the course was fairly easy for me, but this time the series of obstacles involving balance threw me for a loop. I couldn't do them with nearly as much ease. I was stuck on one activity and became the last person across. Something happened to me during the intervening year that laid waste to my confidence. It could have been something biological, psychological, spiritual, or who knows what. I was embarrassed by my performance in front of my classmates.

Luckily, fate gave me another chance to prove myself about two years later when I tackled another survival school confidence course. The balancing obstacles were once again easy for me. The most difficult obstacle required us to pull ourselves across a rope suspended over an Olympic-length pool. I emerged as one of ten people out of two hundred who were successful. I felt like a champion!

So, it is with faith, too. Not everyone is capable of stepping out with confidence into the mystery of life. Some can do it effortlessly while others need two or three attempts. You may need a hundred attempts to get your faith together. No matter. The life of faith is built upon trial and error, developing your faith as you go along with a willingness to meet the faith-building task at hand.

For those who choose to faith up, the promise of freedom found in life is endless.

Learning to Embrace the Unknown

People with exemplary faith embrace the unknown. The unknown does not deter them from acting out the fullness of their hopes and convictions. If you do enough trust falls or even witness a few, it becomes easier to let go. Most fears are overcome by doing what a person fears the most. Whether it is flying in a plane, taking an elevator to the top of a tall building, or learning to swim. The act of bravery is what conquers the fear. Likewise, faith becomes exemplary over time when we do the necessary tasks over and over again. And even then, what you hope for may not come to pass. Those with strong faith keep on moving forward with their hope intact.

This ability to keep moving ahead despite the unknown and the fear lurking inside us is a hallmark of faith.

The psychiatrist Gordon Livingston puts it this way: "To *open* ourselves to other people and new experiences requires a special sort of humility that resists the forces of calcified prejudice." [Emphasis mine.] I believe that Livingston is calling us to live without barriers or enclosures around our view of the world and to embrace new understandings. I love his admonition to let go of preconceptions. Such forces shut down our faith.

The Betrayal of Faith!

Faith, especially at the deepest level, is irrational. It can hardly be treated as a rational formula: if I do this, I will get that. That is how math works. With faith, if you do this, there are chances that you *will* get that, but you may not. I call this the betrayal of faith. It's the side of faith many cannot acknowledge.

I hear many preachers telling adherents that if things don't go the way they hoped, then their faith was not strong enough. I consider this a complete travesty.

This position transforms a reality of faith into a mountain of guilt, shame, and remorse. Instead of acknowledging that sometimes our most profound and intentional hopes do not come to pass, they blame the believer for not faithing well enough. This is a betrayal of faith on another level, and it is wrong. Better to admit that the holy, in his/her infinite wisdom, doesn't always answer every hope and prayer. Or perhaps that desire wasn't meant for them or something even better was coming their way.

I have seen many pastoral counseling clients encounter a betrayal of faith. They typically have done all the right things in life, i.e., maintained an upright, ethical life to the best of their ability, prayed "without ceasing," and maintained a disciplined spiritual practice—but things still didn't work out just quite right. This creates incongruence in their understanding of their faith. Many were taught, or believed, that if they did X (a faith practice or discipline), Y (losing a loved one or encountering a big expense) wouldn't happen. In other words, they'd grown to view their beliefs and practices as prophylaxis against life's struggles. And when that prophylaxis didn't prevent X, their faith often collapsed. Indeed, a loved one who was "called home," and big expenses happen to almost everyone.

Either they weren't prepared for something not to work out, or they didn't experience the expected help from their faith that they imagined. I call this a *betrayal of faith* because these experiences illuminate the gap between expectations and reality. These situations highlight an unknown because one can't know the pain and dissonance found in the gap, until one bumps up against it. Until then, you don't know it exists; you view yourself as immunized by your faith. And once you arrive, you still don't know how long the previously unanticipated and unknown pain will last, another unknown factor. What you do know is that even with all of your faith resources at your disposal, the unknowing is difficult to bear. There is no way around it, either. The beautiful thing is that the more you accustom yourself to confronting and working through unknowns, the less troubling they become.

The Habit of Embracing Mystery

I believe that those with strong faith deal with difficult types of life-threatening and faith-threatening experiences in a superior manner than those who've done little to master their faith. They have worked through such gaps with enough frequency, determination, and perseverance that their faith will not be shaken to the core. Indeed, it may be shaken, but not to its foundations. They've grown to expect that such difficulties and tests will arrive whether they like it or not. The mystery lies in the "when." That is, at what time or point will they show up? They've learned to manage the "what" and "why," and realize the need to have other essential components in place: relationships, practice, and community. Those who typically fall prey to the "betrayal of faith" are those who over-rely on themselves without the other necessary support.

A parishioner named Rocky came to see me after his girlfriend broke up with him. He was devastated. Although Rocky was a devout Muslim, his convictions were difficult to summon up in the aftermath of the breakup. He acknowledged his convictions and beliefs, but really, he just wanted his girlfriend back. A highly reflective individual, he was quite capable of examining his heart and soul for remnants of his faith. During our visits, he realized that "doing" his faith (meditating, coming to acceptance, acknowledging the power of Allah in his life) was appropriate. But he needed more relief from the pain.

Eventually, Rocky began reaching out to family and friends, especially women in his life, to feel connected. He also reconnected with his spiritual community. On their own, none of this could replace the lost relationship or take away the pain, but his faith remained steady. He gradually awakened his resilience, and as the emotional pain subsided, he became more empowered to deal with the unknown future that lay ahead. The pain slowly subsided, but I cannot say with certainty that it completely resolved. Much loss has a way of burrowing into our hearts and souls permanently. Like a condition that goes into remission, we know it is still there, albeit very quietly, and we are never certain it won't come again.

I encouraged Rocky to develop some faith mantras and incorporate other strategies into his daily routine to help him maintain a positive outlook. A faith mantra is any slogan you can remember and repeat to keep you focused on your faith identity, your goals, and to soothe yourself. When I was a doctrinal Christian and struggling with important issues in my life, I would find a few words of scripture and repeat them. It was a means of freeing myself when I found myself entangled in worrisome thoughts. My favorite, when I was in seminary, was Isaiah 12.2, which says, "Truly, God is my salvation; I will trust and not be afraid." The power of the scripture lay in its reminder that I was not alone in my struggle. Repeating the verse has given me something else to focus my attention upon that could replace my worry and anxiety. My negative, life-defeating thoughts were replaced with words that had the power to change me internally. Rather than going through the day with fear, I could take on a trusting mindset, and be confident that God would guide me in the right direction.

The early monastics used the Psalms as a way of focusing the mind. Mantras shift our attention from the pain to something else. They don't take the pain away completely; nothing will. After all, we are human, with functional brains and minds that affect our emotional processes, and we live in the material world where troubles are real. But we do have power over our thoughts if we practice using this power. The monastics employed mantras as a way of transferring mental focus from the self to God.

By the same token, whatever faith system you use, you can train your mind by employing faith mantras to help get you through your struggles. Those with spiritual inclinations can call upon sacred materials and past experiences with the transcendent as a means of refocusing their minds and spirits. Persons with secular leanings can use favorite poems and positive affirmations in the same manner. All of these are equally available and effective for mastering your faith.

Rocky was flooded with thoughts of what he could have done, which "red flags" he had overlooked in his former girlfriend's behavior and things that he could have said that might have changed the outcome of his relationship. This is an endless game of searching, blaming, speculating, and worrying that seldom generates satisfying results. The only results are more worrying, doubting, and increased misery. So, I suggested the story from M. Scott Peck's book, *Further Along the Road Less Traveled* about playing *Monopoly*, a game that can go on interminably until one of the players decides to stop. The moral of the story is that "The only way to stop a game is to stop." I attempted to coach Rocky on how to stop the game. In the end, even that was only a coping strategy for dealing with the pain of loss. It is not a resolution or removal of the suffering. For him, the mystery of how long the pain would linger, or how he'd manage on the road of faith without his partner, or what life held for him down the road, all continued to be mysteries. Faith grows as people in situations such as this accustom themselves to dealing with the pain while holding on to their core convictions, faith practices, and most importantly, staying connected to others in faith-affirming relationships. Rocky slowly began to put his faith into action by meeting new women. His dating life gradually picked up and helped him break through a difficult period of emotional and spiritual suffering.

Faith becomes exemplary when we put it to the test over and over again. In each instance, we face the fact that life has many unknown components that we just can't figure out; life is not a mathematical proof. That is the difference between faith and fact. By maintaining a determined attitude about our faith, even in the face of uncertainty, we slowly make faith a habitual practice.

Chapter 9

Eventually, you become comfortable living with the unknown

If you've ever watched a championship game of any sport, whether it was football, gymnastics, or whatever your favorite may be, you've undoubtedly found yourself marveling at the skills and talents of outstanding athletes. You've probably caught yourself saying, "She sure is lucky to have such natural abilities." Or "I wish I could do that!" Such thoughts are virtually unavoidable when you watch Venus or Serena Williams play tennis or Peyton Manning play football, or even if you watch, say, Ellen DeGeneres conduct an interview on her TV program. They make it look like they were born doing their thing. But we know that in real life that's not how it is. They had to work at it like it was "nobody's business" day-in and day-out. Sure, there are a few child prodigies among us, but the majority of champions or top tier performers hone their crafts by gradually improving over time.

Developing comfort while embracing the unknown—during the mystery of our daily existence—is the same. If you have a mindset of expectation, it will eventually happen for you. The process is not something you can plan or set your alarm clock for. You don't say to yourself, "In two weeks I will be able to embrace mystery like a spiritual guru," then expect to experience that in two weeks. The spiritual life doesn't unfold like that. You *can* say to yourself, "I want to embrace with open arms whatever this day will bring," then begin to live in that openness and allow the day to unfold without resistance.

If you make openness a part of your daily routine, you will eventually find yourself living more freely and less constricted by a need to know or to control every moment.

I encourage you to approach your faith life with determination, to deepen your being by committing yourself to the same work ethic a great athlete would be devoted to. You can commit to putting in the time and effort that leads to competence. While it's impossible to name what the equivalent of a home run might be for you regarding your faith life, I'm confident that when you reach that point, you'll have a deep sense of satisfaction and recognition that you've done it. What makes this complicated is that the goal of obtaining faith and living in mystery is one of life's intangibles. The markers, or evidence of accomplishment are unlike home runs and gold medals. Instead, you are aware of it by an internal awareness that typically only you can see and experience. Still, it is a good practice to put in the effort. Imagining yourself as a spiritual athlete or performer might prepare you for the road and the work ahead.

The story of Dick Allen, a professional baseball player, reminds me of what is entailed when we embrace the mystery of faith. In 1963, Allen became the first black player for the Arkansas Travelers, a minor league team. When word arrived that a black player would be playing on his first night, angry and hostile fans packed the stands to see him. A black man in an all-white sport was an unwelcome sight, and fans hung banners inside and outside the stadium to intimidate Allen. He almost didn't play until he placed a collect phone call to his mother. She told him, "God's given you a talent and a place to show it. If you don't use it, you're being disobedient to me; you're being disobedient to God ...don't let them drive you out." With that, Allen used the next two days to practice, doubling his effort and time in the batter's box. According to the writer William C. Rhoden, "He developed a resolve that would sustain him for the rest of his career." The doubling of time and effort in the life of faith is more difficult to measure, and so are the results, but that is the nature of faith. We have to remain true to our goals and vision for the future and develop the same resolve that Allen summoned up within himself.

If you talk to any person of deep faith about their process of embracing the mystery of life, they'd probably be hard-pressed to describe it. It is a nebulous process, so you have to ask the right questions. Ask them about how they managed to overcome challenges. By doing that, you're more likely to get an earful. Most will love talking about how they learned over time to deal with the difficulties of life and how their faith got them through. They may not put it in terms of an athlete practicing every day, but if you listen closely enough, you'll hear the thread coming through. You must trust the process of becoming whom you aspire to be. The more practice and dedication you have, the more likely it will happen.

Chapter 10

Trusting that the Spirit of Life is always with you

The most unsettling feeling in the world is being alone. In a military environment, the worst-case scenario for a warrior is to be "alone and afraid." The times in my life when I felt the lowest were usually when I felt separated from friends, family, and God. Those were also the times when I had to remind myself to draw on my faith. By calling upon my faith and trust in the spirit of life, I was able to overcome feelings of loneliness. But most importantly, I could remind myself that the trouble would eventually pass and trust in the hopeful future that was surely on the horizon (if I could only open my eyes wide enough to see it). Even when faith exemplars *feel* alone, they know deep inside that a transcendent power greater than themselves is leading the way. Two factors are at work here: trust and a type of knowing. Let's explore each more closely.

When we use the word "trust," ultimately, we are saying, "be confident." Trusting is an orientation that says to the self, "go forward without fear." Your inner compass guides you with certainty that it can be counted on, just as travelers in the wilderness count on the North Star to lead them when in darkness. When you have trust in your heart and soul, you can move through the world confidently and with assurance. Your predisposition to trust becomes your inner compass. This is not to say that every situation will go down in the books as a victory or a perfect outcome. But whatever the outcome, you will be able to withstand it because of your confidence that the universe has prepared you for each moment.

One woman I knew in a former congregation seemed to have a perpetually open spirit, always radiating warmth and love from within. I knew Mary had dealt with difficult times. After losing her husband she had to manage her daily needs on a meager income. I sat down with her on occasion for brief chats, after the mid-week service, to ascertain how she was handling it all. I'll never forget her story of "deliverance," shortly after her husband died unexpectedly. She was running short on money and didn't know how she'd make her mortgage that month. She continued praying and trusting that the money would arrive. Then, just before the due date, she learned that her husband had taken out an insurance policy she wasn't aware of. That, combined with an extension granted by the mortgage company, got her through just in time. She told me that throughout the whole ordeal she never doubted that God (or the universe) would provide a way for her. That form of trust comes from the experience of being "delivered" over and over again. For some of us, deliverance may not come as readily. But do not let that derail your faith. Keep on the journey of believing.

What distinguishes people of strong faith from others is the self-reinforcing memory of deliverance from the last time it had shown its bounty. They remember the previous experience of overcoming a difficult time and use that memory to reinforce their confidence going into the next situation. On the other hand, people without seasoned faith usually do not remember the last time. And even if they do remember, they are unable to see it enough to harness the power and generate faith. Consequently, they are often thrown into a state of despair, anxiety, and fear. People like Mary don't allow themselves to fall into the trap of forgetting. The reinforcement of experience is always present in their lives and available to them.

Over time, people like Mary had spread their faith and resilience to others. In the African American church, they become known as "church mothers," or for men, "brother so-and-so." They live up to this title because:

1) They've shared their faith narrative with everyone they encounter, and often quite publicly through testimony before the congregation or community.

2) They're always present at their church or spiritual community, which reinforces their trust in the life of faith. Their constant presence also reinforces others' trust in them. Being around people like this is contagious. Their spirit rubs off on others, who then begin living into their sense of trust. Equally important is the level of credibility these people possess. You know that their faith is a result of being tested over time, as they've gone through rough patches and came out on the other side to tell about it. Their narratives reflect their real-life experience in such a way that they radiate integrity, so others can trust them.

What they *know* about the life of faith is a different type of knowledge than the empirical, although it is empirical in a spiritual way. Empirical experience is reproducible: if one person does the same thing as another they will achieve the same results. What one person of strong faith can do, another can do, but the method is more individual and contains broader strokes.

Reproducing the same results is done in the laboratory of life, not in a lab full of beakers and measurements. Over time, we learn that life has a way of testing us all.

After periods of spiritual discovery, both quantitative and qualitative, we've come to know that the spirit of life and power deep within us have conspired to help us become who we are. This becomes a spiritual fact of life, and thus, a spiritual form of knowledge.

In their book *Soul Theology*, African American theologians Nicholas Cooper-Lewter and Henry Mitchell provide a key insight into this way of knowing. In their system of "soul theology," persons of faith affirm in their being a fundamental understanding that they will "endure and persevere in their identity and faith." The authors put it this way:

People do not have to surrender to the pressures of life and give up in despair. If there is one test to which every system of belief should be subjected, it is this: the test of its ability to sustain and empower believers and to help them cope with life. No degree of orthodoxy can compensate for a deficiency in this aspect.

Knowledge of this sort is life-giving and affirming, delivering the hope and conviction that our life means something, and inspires us to maintain a faith-filled orientation toward life and all that it sends our way. No matter what, we don't abandon our identity as people of faith, nor our trust that the universe will forever be on our side, and by our side. Another way to establish this is knowing that the spirit of life, God, the sacred presence of nature, or the universe is forever lighting and guiding our paths.

Chapter 11

Committing significant energy to the three re-enforcers of sustaining faith

For faith to take hold in your life, you need to commit to living faithfully. By faithfully, I mean you need to make a conscious effort, or a pledge within your being to focus your energy in that direction. What we do with intention and repetition we eventually master. Perhaps it is easier to reflect on the opposite action. If you imagine a person who is trying to quit smoking or drinking, you know that they will be required to exert significant energy and attention to things that distract them from cigarettes or alcohol. The drive to smoke or drink is quite powerful, and quitting is unlikely to happen on its own. According to AA, the habit will be broken by an intention to let go of the cravings and trusting that a power greater than ourselves can remove it. Recovery from addiction begins with a conscious effort or pledge to rehabilitate oneself to a new state. A similar commitment, or energy, is required of the one who wants to grow in faith.

I'd like to re-emphasize what can reinforce getting a hold of your faith: sustaining relationships, participating in a faith community, and participating in regular spiritual practices, whether that's spending time in nature or more formal practices. Each of these reinforces your commitment to growing your faith in the way you want it to be. You don't need to limit yourself to these three, but I am convinced that you will require these practices to reach your goal. My research has demonstrated that people with the most resilient faith reinforce these habits in their lives.

In most cases, finding these practices happened naturally. That is, they hadn't decided to make these reinforcers a part of their lives; it just happened through the normal course of living. In other cases, people seeking strong faith were at the right place at the right time, surrounded by good people who encouraged them on their journey. Either way, these reinforcers were considered to be the most important ones.

The benefit to you is that you don't have to figure out what might grow your faith from square one. If you continue to remind yourself that these three supports are active in your life, and trust that this is the foundation of solid faith, I hope that you will begin living as a person of strong faith.

Sustaining Relationships With Family, Friends, Faith Mentors, and Role Models

Looking back over the course of my ministry, it is easy to see a "cloud of witnesses" that helped me along the way. Some were quite foundational and helped me see my gifts and graces for the work of ministry. Others kind of prodded me here and there. Many taught me by modeling excellent ministry themselves. Then, some people supplied tons of applause and stood by me to celebrate various milestones as I reached them.

It helps when your family is on your side. Whether it is your parents, spouse, siblings, children, cousins, or grandparents. Having your family on board for your faith journey gives you a natural boost of energy and confirmation that you are on the right track. After all, they are the ones who tend to know you best. Family can include extended family, of course. It all depends on how *you* define family. Persons of faith often include their "worship family" or spiritual community because they spend so much time together. There is also the notion of being "born again,"[4] which tends to signify that you've been grafted onto a new faith family, which comes with your new birth. However, you designate such relationships, the key is: these are people who sustain you. They satisfy your need for solid, trustworthy, and dependable relationships.

There is a fine line between family and friends. The line can be quite blurred, to say the least. As you get older, you gain more appreciation for sustaining friendships, and bloodlines often matter less than faithfulness. Your best friends are often the ones you depend on as your faith grows. There's something inherent about the faithing process that lends itself to relying more on friends than family. This has to do with maturity and recognizing that you can trust people who treat you *like* family because over time your relationships have grown to support such a description. After all, what is marriage but a family created between two people who were once strangers, who by law and protocol remain biologically unrelated to one another. Yet, the bond they create and the love they have for one another can be stronger than any blood ties.

In such friendships, you can find the energy needed to sustain your faith. That is why it is important and essential to nurture

---

4   The term born again has roots in the Christian faith, but it need not be relegated solely to a Christian meaning. It is a metaphor that can be used by you regardless of your faith orientation. Another way of understanding born again might be constructing a "new you."

your friendships. People strong in their faith, however, realize that such friendships are a two-way street. You maintain the relationships not just for what you get from them, but also for what you contribute to your friend's wellbeing. You have probably encountered people who seemed to be your acquaintances for selfish reasons only. Such one-sided relationships have a draining quality—they sap you of emotional and spiritual energy. After a few of these negative encounters, you can recognize this type of person a mile away. If you don't protect yourself, such experiences can destroy your faith in people. True friendships strengthen your faith by deepening your trustfulness in people. As you grow to trust people to be there for you, to be committed to their word, to allow yourself to be there for them, and as you mutually allow each other into your intimate worlds, your faith grows. The seeds of faith will begin flowering and pollinating your world in miraculous ways.

Friends come in many varieties I've discovered over the years. There will be some people you meet and immediately recognize the possibility of friendship. Others not so much. The writer Robert J. Wicks suggests that we ought to be intentional about our friendship circles and be sure that we have four specific types of friends to maintain "A sense of perspective, openness, and balance." Let's explore each of these closely because each one has real value for faith development.

Prophets

The first type of friend is the *prophet*, whose special role in your life is encouraging you to live honestly and truthfully, without avoiding necessary suffering. We encounter experiences every day that force us to make difficult decisions. The prophets in our life tell us not to avoid the pain or discomfort if it means living with integrity and truthfulness. They remind us that the truth will set us free. As Wicks puts it, "To seek comfort in lieu of the truth may mean that to avoid pain, we will also avoid responding to opportunities of real value, real life." Growing your faith will often involve working through pain in its various forms. You gradually realize that even pain and suffering have value in your life.

Cheerleaders

The next type of friend is the *cheerleader*. Personally, this is my favorite because I tend to be this type of friend, and also because I've benefitted so much from the cheerleaders in my life. Luckily, my parents were two of my cheerleaders. From them and others like them, I realized that I could do almost anything I set my mind to do. Wicks views cheerleaders as a counterbalance to the prophetic friend. Cheerleaders, he says, supply us with the "Unabashed, enthusiastic, unconditional acceptance" that we all need. We may take for granted the necessity for this type of friend, but we do that to our peril. This group of friends helps deal with difficulties, and they inspire us to take calculated risks and believe in us when we do. Those same people will be the ones you need if things turn out differently than you've expected, and you need someone you can depend on.

Harassers

The next group of friends is the *harassers*. These are the ones who keep you from taking yourself too seriously. They show you how to laugh at yourself and your foibles, which you can easily overlook, and sometimes deny. Someone good about laughing at himself was former President George W. Bush. His self-deprecating humor showed that he had a down-to-earth human side. To me, he seemed genuine, and I've learned to adopt this as a way of taking myself a notch down when a part of me may be seeking higher ground from a sense of righteousness. History shows that self-deprecation hit a high mark in 1906 when the singer Bert Williams hit it big with his record "Nobody." Some of the lyrics were:

"I ain't never done nothin' to nobody /

I ain't never got nothin' from nobody, no time /

And until I get somethin' from somebody, sometime /

I'll never do nothin' for nobody, no time."

The lyrics have a different sensibility to modern ears, but the idea remains the same. Vulnerability and laughing at yourself need not be considered taboo. Instead, we can welcome such introspection—even if it comes from a harasser. Until such a practice becomes instinctive, or if you find that you just can't pull it off yourself, it's good to keep a harasser close by to keep yourself in check. This type of friend can also help us avoid emotional burnout, which sometimes results from having unrealistic expectations for ourselves or a high self-regard. The tendency to cajole us lightly is often the perfect counter-balance for those who tend to take themselves too seriously.

Guides

The last type of friend is the *guide*—perhaps the most important type of friend for faith development. Guides tend to do a lot of deep listening, and they understand the difference between what we say or do, and our intentions. Theologian Robert Wicks in his book, *Bounce*, puts it this way: "They search and look for nuances in what we share with them to help us to uncover some of the 'voices' that are unconsciously guiding our lives, especially the ones that make us hesitant, anxious, fearful, and willful." This Guide describes a friend who has a deep concern for others as people full of potential and growth. Having such a person in your inner circle is vital if you are to master your faith because, without consciousness about your own inner life, you're guaranteed to be ruled by unconscious voices of your own or bad advice from other people, rather than mastering what kind of input is spiritually sound.

A friend serving as a guide may also be a mentor. When we think of mentors, we recall people who have taken us under their wing to show us the way with a clearer perspective. A *mentor* has a specific purpose and also creates an environment where learning can take place. It is quite common for ministers to have mentors as they go through seminary in their first few years of ministry. The mentor-protégé relationship is often formally arranged by someone with a specific interest in helping a junior partner learn under an experienced teacher. However, it need not be a formal arrangement, since a mentoring relationship can emerge from unscheduled contact between the parties. Either way, the mentor's role is to facilitate growth and learn to develop a deeper faith.

It is important to choose a mentor who has considerable experience, integrity, and commitment to a life of faith. The adult development and learning specialist, Lois Zachary, argues that, above all, good mentors understand their journey. They have "self-awareness, which is triggered by self-reflection ... an ability to understand the mentee's journey ... and perspective." Typically, such people are easy to identify by their faith walk— the congruency between what they say and do. We call this "walking the walk and talking the talk." A mentor needs to be able to do both. One without the other might result in a protégé having a non-optimal experience. My father left the church because he felt the ministers in his childhood did not live the way they preached. Choosing a mentor requires time and careful consideration. Even then, some mentor-protégé relationships don't work out for various reasons, in which case, you must continue your search for another.

By the same token, a protégé seeking to grow their faith will benefit the most from a mentor when they are open to listening and learning. You must keep your heart and mind open to the wisdom of the mentor. Often you will agree, other times you won't. But unless the mentor is asking you to do something illegal, dangerous, or lacking in integrity, it's wise to reflect deeply on the mentor's counsel as you incorporate their advice and suggestions into your way of being. Those unwilling to follow in the footsteps of their mentors may not be ready for outside advice.

I've spoken earlier in a lengthy section about role models and their importance in the life of faith. My sole reason for mentioning this again is that the importance of role models simply cannot be overstated. Even exemplars of faith need a constant supply of role models to carry them along and help them remain on the straight and narrow.

This point is reinforced by a story about the great evangelist, the Reverend Billy Graham. When he traveled, he required every person in his entourage to have an "accountability partner," who made sure that his partner didn't get into trouble while on the road. Now, one would think that people in Rev. Graham's entourage had been hand-picked to serve with him, and had been chosen based on his or her demonstrated integrity and witness as a person of faith. Still, Rev. Graham insisted that each person have another person of equal character looking out for them in a sort of mentoring capacity. This goes to show that one can never be so upright to exclude good mentors who continue to serve as spiritual guides, or accountability partners, along the journey of faith.

Participating in a Community of Faith

Being in a community of faith helps keep one grounded in relationships of shared values and norms, or established ways of practice and being. These are primary relationships established with the spirit of life or whatever the community deems its most transcendent value or aspiration. I've described life in a faith community as both a social and theological event because the community promotes communion with God or divine spirit in both interpersonal communications and relationships. As people interact with one another through speech and service, they spread certain standards about what constitutes a good life and ethical behavior. In many spiritual communities, this is referred to as a covenant, or an agreement, about how people choose to join together.

Over time, how one lives in community begins to permeate the whole of one's life. What you do in your faith community should be consistent with how you live in your other communities. The key is striving for consistency. Because communities of faith, at their best, tend to promote the highest of spiritual values, such as love, compassion, forgiveness, and mutual care. A person who gets a hold of their faith would be carrying the values of the faith community with them and sharing those values with everyone they meet along the way.

When we don't see congruency in a person's walk and talk, we tend to question the integrity of the community and the individual. The mark of a life-affirming faith community might be that its members embody faith values as they move out into the world beyond their chosen community, interacting with neighbors, recreational teams, sharing self-improvement pastimes such as Toastmasters, and, of course, meeting new friends. In a faith community, it takes a considerable amount of time for each member to integrate communal faith values into their lives. Members must make a conscious effort to embody the values and covenants of their community. We tend to regard that people who are models of faith are also masters of the process of give and take and letting others do the same.

Incorporating Spiritual Practices

When it comes to faith development and expanding your deep faith, spiritual practices are the primary lifeline. Like all disciplines, spiritual or not, a person practicing consistently eventually performs better. Faith is no exception. If you only engage in spiritual practices when you feel like it, when time permits, or after all of your other priorities are squared away, it would be unreasonable to expect to have any spiritual muscles when you need them. Instead, you'll find your muscles flaccid and wielding negligible power when facing difficult times in your life. It is important to incorporate spiritual practices into your daily routine and maintain discipline as you train.

If we look at the human being as a vessel designed to receive the blessings of life, we can understand the need we all have to be filled with God's spirit.

To be filled up, however, we often need to empty ourselves of our "stuff." Spiritual practice is a means of emptying ourselves of our baggage, or issues (whatever word works best for you) to create room for the gifts of the spirit. By engaging in the spiritual practice of contemplation, for example, we open up space within ourselves to receive spiritual gifts. Having this space is important for faith to prosper because it helps us see how we can shape our development.

A similar way of imagining having space for faith to grow comes from the writer Joyce Rupp in her book *The Cup of Our Life.* She affirms that our empty coffee mug symbolizes our empty, or hollow, selves, while a filled cup symbolizes our thirst for the spirit. The ritual of filling a cup, drinking from it, emptying it, and cleaning it begins the process all over again. Thus symbolizing our ordinary experiences as we seek to have our thirst quenched. As Rupp writes:

"A cup is a container for holding something. Whatever it holds has to eventually be emptied so that something more can be put into it. I have learned that I cannot always expect my life to be full. There has to be some emptying, some pouring out, if I am to make room for the new. The spiritual journey is like that—a constant process of emptying and filling, of giving and receiving, of accepting and letting go."

As Rupp sees it, she encourages the use of the cup as a way of visualizing a daily practice of prayer. I appreciate her method because what is often perceived as a complex process of spiritual practices has been turned into a practical application we all can use to guide our lives. Many of us will, by default, allow our spiritual practice to drift off-center. This method helps us make our spiritual walk a focal point in our lives. She astutely highlights the importance of regular practice, but goes even further, saying our spiritual life "Involves all of our life, every moment of our existence."

Getting a hold of our faith is about recognizing that our whole life is a spiritual practice. Being conscious of this is a distinguishing mark of people with a mature faith.

So far, I have not laid out *what* the actual spiritual practices are. There are many. We will address these in more detail later in the book. For now, let us name a few. Most of us are familiar with, or have a regular practice of prayer, meditation, and reading sacred literature (such as the Bible, Tanakh, Bhagavad Gita, Koran, etc..) We also attend worship or engage in group practice such as chanting or Quaker meetings. Many faith communities and churches offer a communal Bible study. Others have a Buddhist sangha for people to attend regularly. Other faiths have meetings in people's homes, a means of building a spiritual community within the larger community. All of these are excellent ways to develop your faith muscles with other people as companions.

SECTION III

MYSTICISM AS A PATH TO FAITH THAT WORKS

Chapter 12

Demystifying mysticism

Now we turn our attention to the actual process of growing in the life of faith through spiritual practices, and in particular, the practices of the mystics. I admit right away that when I heard the word *mysticism*, my mind imagined a monk sitting alone in a cold monastery with nothing but his thoughts to keep him company. With this mental picture comes an assumption that he is in that cell for hours with a mandate to purify his thoughts by reciting the Psalms and meditating only on God. The words *ascetic* and *punishment* also arise in my mind. You may have similar thoughts and might be considering skipping this chapter. Let me assure you right now that is not what this chapter is about. Not at all! What I do have in mind is much more appealing and suitable for the everyday person who wants to grow in faith and have a life! So, relax and prepare to join the ranks of those close to God—the spirit of life—or if you will, the transcendent mystery that binds us one to the other.

The "What" of Mysticism

When we talk about mysticism, we simply refer to a form of religious experience that combines a deep relationship with the transcendent and spiritual practice as a means of expanding ordinary living. A *mystic* is a person who has declared that s/he has had a direct encounter with God, or a life-shaping experience in the natural world, which they are compelled to share with others. There is no requirement per se that mystics report their experiences. But often, mystics write about their encounters of spirit with vivid imagery. In other words, mystics have personal transcendent experiences that turn out to be so profound that they feel compelled to share them with us. A person who chooses non-God language may have an intense encounter or transcendent moment in the presence of other human beings that seems beyond ordinary, day-to-day experience. Often at the heart of mystical experience is a deep sense of connecting with the other on a deeply intimate level. In the aftermath of such encounters, you might feel as though two spirits—two souls— have met face-to-face. Some report having become one with the sacred power that binds us together.

Down through the ages, mystics have dedicated their lives to sustaining an ongoing encounter with the Holy. For some, this mystical experience is a vocation in and of itself, as if being outside of mystical experience is akin to being out of touch with all that is Holy. All religious and spiritual traditions have their mystics. In Islam, there are Sufis. The word "Sufi" means *purity* and reflects the pious nature of Sufis as they pursue their relationship with the sacred. Within Buddhism, the Madhyamaka tradition focuses on the Middle Way, a teaching of the Buddha. In Hinduism, we find the spiritual practices of chanting and yoga, which aim to quiet the mind as a path to perfect peace. Yogis often seek a mystical state as an outcome of their spiritual discipline. The Fourth Way arose from Western esotericism, and advocates concentrating on mind, body, and emotions as a means of maximizing wakefulness, or consciousness. This tradition might be considered utilitarian because practitioners use their heightened mystical awareness in the here and now, not for the sake of drawing closer to the sacred.

Mystics became known, when, in the aftermath of their heightened "awareness of meeting God," they taught others how they might seek similar experiences. Having stumbled upon the Great Mystery, and being *known* and *accepted* (while knowing that many spiritual people *wished* for such an encounter) mystics have pulled back the curtain on their lives to show us that such encounters are available to everyone. The bestseller lists and movie theaters are full of stories about people who have reported these experiences. We recognize the mystics because they've been enlightened and wrote to tell their experience. What tends to set mystics apart is the language and clarity of expression they use to describe their experiences. Their writings convey deep connection by shaping a mystical genre, which many identify as purely religious and spiritual experiences.

We should keep in mind that what the mystics and people of strong faith have in common is the discipline, or practice, of exercising their faith muscles regularly, over long periods. This prepares them to seamlessly shift into the mystical realm when the metaphorical door to the sacred opens. What we hear and read about in their journals, then, is the result of developed awareness and listening for the transcendent, which results in their ability to experience that source of power directly and respond accordingly. Let me put it this way: there is a saying that when one door closes, another opens. You, too, can prepare yourself for these mystical experiences by practicing your spiritual discipline frequently and with intention. That way, when the door opens that permits you to shift from the mundane experience to the mystical, you will be ready to enter. This is the key: when you are adequately prepared, when your heart and spirit are sufficiently open, a transforming and sustaining love will engulf you. If you are not ready to step into a new type of experience, the door will close, leaving you on the outside! Chances are that another opportunity will arise, but why put yourself through the wait, regret, and anticipation? Practicing your discipline with regularity, whether it's praying, meditating, or being in nature, readies you for when the opportunity presents itself.

The "Why" of Mysticism

Mystics, like others who have a hold of their faith, describe their faith journeys in ways that identify striving to live by the will of the Great Mystery. Others may describe the journey as being in touch with the deepest values of life. Traditions such as Hinduism and Buddhism, as I understand it, lie somewhere in between. Mystics from these traditions are usually led by deep inner wisdom or transcendent values. When they speak, we hear their steadfast connection and relationship to their faith community as they call others to cultivate a practice of deep spiritual listening in their own lives.

The core emphasis on being in the right relationship with one's faith community versus practicing in isolation is why mysticism is a mainstay in the heart of the faithing process. The Unitarian Universalist mystic, Tom Owen-Towle, reinforces this notion in his book, *Freethinking Mystics with Hands*, by saying, "Relationality is religion's primary paradigm, insinuating that wisdom is uncovered not in me or you, but between us—in possibilities that yet transcend us."

This section of the book focuses on how you can implement mystic-like religious practices in your own life. We'll do this by exploring in-depth the many facets of mysticism and the mystical life. In the next section, we will examine spiritual disciplines you can integrate into your spiritual tool kit to grow and master your faith and spiritual practice. Most of these disciplines were used by mystics and other faith leaders to continually grow and master their faith, as we strive to do.

I'm convinced that each of us can master this experience in our own lives. As the writer Alan Altany in his work titled "What Makes a Mystic," states, mysticism "Is not only for an elite group of super-holy people. Women and men, young and old, celibate and married, rich and poor, educated and illiterate, famous and unknown, saints and sinners have experienced this transformative presence of God in their lives." Each of us has the capacity for a mystical experience according to our definition. In this chapter, we are especially interested in how everyday people of faith, that is, those who have mystical qualities deeply embedded in their lives, use their faith during life's difficulties and challenges.

As part of our journey together, we will explore the writings of the African American mystic, Howard Thurman (1899 to 1981), whose experiences of mysticism greatly shaped my understanding of spiritual practice.

Thurman, an ordained minister, educator, mediator, and advisor to leaders, identified with everyday people. He had a favorite expression that conveyed his affection for people involved in the day-to-day struggle—those with "their backs are against the wall." In reality, all of us have had difficulties, prompting us to draw upon our faith when dealing with the death of a spouse or significant other, losing a job, encountering trauma, or managing depression. These are major life events. Sometimes, however, it is the day-to-day grind that calls us to live out our deepest faith commitments—working at a boring job, dealing with a demanding boss, struggling with bills and creditors, taking care of a sick or aging family member, or a child with disabilities. All of these demands keep our backs against the wall. In the rest of this section, I will show how mysticism worked for Thurman and how it also influenced me on my path. Then, we'll explore some spiritual disciplines more intensively, giving examples of how you can implement them to live more fully, whether your back is against the wall, or you are running toward the finish line.

Chapter 13

Personal Experiences of Mysticism

In his pamphlet *Mysticism and the Experience of Love*, Howard Thurman described mysticism as "The response of the individual to a personal encounter with God within his spirit." Thurman claimed that there is "God within." For him, the divine, or the divine spirit, lives inside of us continuously. Still, it is our individual responsibility to become aware of it and hear that still voice more clearly. He added weight to this idea in his book, *The Creative Encounter*, stating, "The *central* fact in religious experience is the awareness of meeting God." If you are of a different theological persuasion, try not to let the God-language distract you. Just concentrate on the action. I believe that it is *hearing* and *awareness* that mystics and others with strong faith experience transcendence and the universe directly by going deeper with their faith. As Thurman says,

> "The descriptive words are varied: sometimes it is called an encounter; sometimes, a confrontation; and sometimes, a sense of presence. What is insisted upon, however, without regard to the term used, is that in the experience defined as religious, the individual is seen as being exposed to direct knowledge of ultimate meaning in which all that the individual is, becomes clear as an immediate and often distinct revelation."

In other words, it is not so much the words you choose to describe the encounter as much as your personal experience itself that becomes the focus. Having the encounter is what matters most. You want assurance that you've felt the presence of ultimate expression or have had a meaningful experience of the natural world in the here and now. The ultimate is right here, right now with you.

The spirit of life is saying that as you seek out the spirit, that same spirit is seeking you.

Thurman borrowed four characteristics of the mystical experience from Charles A. Bennett's *A Philosophical Study of Mysticism*. Mystics-to-be may view these characteristics as guidelines or suggestions for monitoring your own experience. As a beginner or a continuing practitioner, you need not feel pressure to incorporate each element. Instead, use them as a way of understanding what a full range of experience might be. First, you experience "a revelation of truth." The revealed truth is less a hidden secret than a plain view of "the inside," or a clear picture of the divine. Second, you become aware that the experience of the divine is not a unique occurrence. It has happened before to many people, yet, for the mystic, each occurrence is considered a "rediscovery of the eternal." Third, the experience enables you to conform your will to divine will. Thurman described the divine as "An object of love." In other words, during a mystical experience, you will discover God as your object of love. In Shakespearean terms, you could say that God is your "Betrothed." For the non-theist, you might say that you are conformed to your ultimate values or meaning. Finally, the mystical encounter with the divine is a total experience. That is to say, as a mystic, you encounter the truth as a unified whole: the experience is neither indistinct nor fragmented. The invitation here is to keep these elements of mystical experience in the back of your mind as a framework from which to build your own spiritual experience.

If this all sounds, well, too *mystical* to you, try to imagine the process as a way of making the mysterious aspects of spiritual practice more human. I believe this is where *Unitarian Universalism may provide an anchor. UU theology focuses on the human element of religious experience.* Faith from this perspective happens not "out there" in the heavens or beyond our earthly existence, but right here in time and space between you and I as we create relationships and communities. Human hands and hearts are the conduits for the manifestation of transcendent experience. As I encounter you, you encounter me, and between us, we usher in the presence of the sacred. By making a mental substitution between *the divine other* and the *human* being *(I, you, us)*, hopefully, the mystical process will come together and open up more possibilities for your faithing experience.

Chapter 14

An Inside Look at Mystical Experiences

Thurman provides glimpses into his personal mystical experience in his writings. Sometimes these occurred while he was walking in nature, in the woods as a young boy, or near the ocean in his adult life. During those times, Thurman found himself overcome by feelings of utter serenity and profound stillness. Most of us have probably experienced something similar. According to the scholar Carlyle Fielding Stewart in his book, *God, Being, and Liberation*, Thurman regarded nature as a "Constant companion" and an "Important theological source. For him, "No other element of life is as replete and improvisational in its intimation of life's ranging possibilities." At times when amid natural elements, Thurman reported a sense of unity when "The environment and what was emerging inside of [him] became one." Thurman's language lets us know that he had established contact with the transcendent, a type of mystery beyond himself. For persons of humanist, or perhaps, earth-centered faith traditions, Thurman's experience might be particularly resonant.

For a more specific account of Thurman's mystical experiences, we turn to his story of a meeting with a group of Canadian Indian chiefs. In his autobiography, *With Head and Heart*, he says,

"My words went forth, but they seemed to strike an invisible wall, only to fall back to meet other words flowing from my mouth. The tension was unbearable. Then, suddenly, as if by some kind of magic, the wall vanished, and I had the experience of sensing an organic flow of meaning passing between them and me. It was as if we had dropped into a continuum of communication that existed *a priori* long before human speech was formed into sounds and symbols."

What is so striking in this account is Thurman's direct reliance upon relationship as the means for connecting with the transcendent, reminding us of Owen-Towle's description. A close reading of his account reveals that together with others, he sensed a communion beyond ordinary relationship. Indeed, it was the gathering of people that initiated the "Organic flow" and "Continuum of communication," that established the mystical quality of the moment. Through these phrases, Thurman harmonized thought and speech, making them into a unified form of communication. In doing so, he cut to the heart of mystical experience and demonstrated the heightened sensitivity to the unseen presences and processes of our human commonality that engages in sympathy, mindfulness, and spirit.

Now, you might wonder, how would I know that I'm having a mystical experience? This presents a problem for mystics, because, like all of us, they are limited by their ability to describe their experiences in words. The mystical experience happens internally, where words might be lacking. Moreover, mystical experience is not usually amenable to empirical evidence, although many have sought data to validate such experiences. Thurman resolved this dilemma by recognizing that one's claim to experiencing ultimate meaning is "inherent and frontal in him

[and] is also inherent and frontal in life." In other words, what is natural to the inner life is vital to all life. What occurs naturally within our inner life (feelings, emotions, physical changes, and bodily sensations) can be trusted as evidence that you are front-and-center in the presence of the Holy. If you sense from within yourself that you are having a transcendent moment, trust that it is so! You need no one else to validate your experience for you. Nor do you need to compare your experience to another's. This is what mastering your faith is all about.

As you encounter the divine on an inner deeper level, your external encounter with life should follow suit. Working with this interpretation of Thurman, it becomes clearer that mysticism need not be an elusive experience; instead, it is quite human and deeply life-affirming. By learning to trust your internal spiritual experience, however, you define and live by it and gradually grow into living a deep and satisfying life of faith.

<h1 style="text-align:center">Chapter 15</h1>

Mysticism for All, Regardless of Religious Tradition

Again, I'd like to emphasize that the language of mysticism is broad enough to include several religious and spiritual traditions. The phrase "ultimate concern" is used by many theologians for describing what many call "God," but in secular language. This can be expressed with several terms: The sacred spirit of life and love, "something bigger than ourselves," a higher power or of course the Holy, and many more. We might say that we can practice openness in our language with confidence, knowing that it is meant to point us to a "religion of the inner light."

This theologically-neutral language allows us to build bridges and find common ground among mystics of various traditions, preferencing none above the others. Many you may encounter will find this approach distasteful, arguing that if you don't stand for something specific, meaning the divine expressed in classic sacred texts, such as the Bible or Torah, your spiritual practice will be weak and built upon sinking sand. I strongly disagree and see such arguments as defense mechanisms. Don't allow yourself to be drawn into such arguments or confrontations. The true mark of strong faith is your capacity to live out your convictions and values using your spiritual language and practices with confidence and strength. This is a valuable takeaway from

Thurman and what sets him apart as a teacher of exemplary faith. By using a universal language, he invites people from all faith traditions to experience their firsthand knowledge of the "inner light" and make it their own. No religious tradition is superior to another. All people can encounter their faith.

Origins of the Faith Instinct

To what might we attribute Thurman's early religious development and sensitivity? Did he have special gifts or spiritual practices, or was he merely awake to such experiences? It seems that he made use of his inner resources, the same resources that each of us has within us waiting to come alive. He wrote about these developments in *With Head and Heart*:

> "Years ago I had made a tentative discovery when I preached for the first time in the Methodist Church in my hometown and, to my amazement, discovered that I had the same kind of religious experience there that I had in my own Baptist Church. Now, in India, there was a redefining of that experience, only in a much more complex and subtle way...I had to find my way to the place where I could stand side by side with a Hindu, a Buddhist, a Moslem (*sic*), and know that the authenticity of his experience was identical with the essence and authenticity of my own."

As a Unitarian Universalist with an appreciation for many religious traditions, I am struck by how Thurman takes this approach without limiting himself to his Christian perspective. What struck me was his ability to step outside of his tradition, what I'd call his own *bias*, and open his heart to other ways of spiritual practice. And at such an early age! Although he strays outside traditional historical biblical linguistic concepts, he remains within the broader context of God-language while using concrete Christian imagery and many illustrations drawn directly from the Bible. This inclusive approach to being within what he considered to be God's will while seeking a multi-dimensional approach to religious experience, corresponds directly with our definition of people who've got a hold of their faith That is, his multi-dimensional approach and language match up with the characteristics we've listed earlier: people with strong faith. Moreover, Thurman's ability to see God from various faith traditions adds a dimension that we seldom witness outside interfaith dialogue.

Thurman raises a high bar for both mystical experience and true faith. We cannot simply stay in our small world and consider that to be living our deepest faith. This is a call to strive for an open-ended and open-hearted type of faith and spiritual experience, which is difficult to attain. In my daily life, I sometimes find myself being critical of other faiths, especially those that are so concrete about their own faith lives. I am aware of my own bias at these times and I do comprehend that I continually need to live out the teachings of Thurman and other great teachers. I also realize that aspiring to strong faith is a discipline and practice that I might not master right away. But I continue to open my heart as I remain aware of my desire to grow, extend lovingkindness, and soften my judgments.

I continually strive to find a prophetic voice that calls people to be their truest selves in the world. As I do this, I challenge myself to preserve integrity in my spiritual practice and everyday living. That is true for me as I write this book. Knowing that I have a broad audience, I aim to be respectful of all traditions, privileging none above the others, while acknowledging that the bulk of my experience—like Thurman's—is from the African American Christian tradition.

I have been influenced by many other traditions as well, for which I am deeply grateful.

Chapter 16

The Transformative Power of Mysticism

For Thurman, the experience of knowing God inwardly unlocks significant meaning; yet gaining that meaning is not the ultimate end. Through knowing God as he wrote about in *The Inward Journey*, the mystic "Senses that he is being dealt with at a center in himself that goes beyond all of his virtues and vices." Not only does the experience of God transcend all their other experiences; it "Meets the deepest need of his life." It is so powerful and all-encompassing that the mystic wants to share it with others so they too can grow in awareness of the range and possibility of religious experience. While I view this desire as inherent to mysticism, it applies to other practitioners as well, as they share their faith narrative with anyone they encounter. It is a story too big to hold inside.

Thurman contends that this is the essence of experiencing God's love. It remains total, fulfilling, and pervasive throughout a person's life, as long as we maintain sensitiveness (Thurman's term) to God's presence. Walter Fluker, the Thurman scholar, argues that "The inner life is primary to 'world consciousness'; i.e., the internality of experience informs the externality of existence." This means that our inner experience of the transcendent working within us has a direct bearing on our experience of the world. So, we're encouraged to seek religious experience not solely for the sake of our individual spiritual needs. We can allow this inner experience to guide our sense of direction and purpose for being in the world. When we peer into our inner lives from this perspective, we might see that it connects with our life's mission for our own sake, our community, and the world beyond.

The Meaning of Sensitiveness

There is more to this concept of mysticism that is valuable for our understanding here: the experience of being sensitive, or having *sensitiveness*, is a term that Thurman derived from the Apostle Paul's Letter to the Philippians in the New Testament. There we find Paul writing, "And it is my prayer that your love may be more and more rich in knowledge and all manner of insight, enabling you to have a sense of what is vital..." (vv. 1.9-10) [*Emphasis added.*] Thurman's brilliant comeback to Paul's prayer adds another dimension to the mystical life, and therefore, the life of strong believers. He says his book, *Deep is the Hunger*, "To have a sense of what is vital, a basic and underlying awareness of life and its potentialities at every level of experience, this is to be an Apostle of Sensitiveness." From this definition, we can infer that for those among us who have this sensitiveness, all life can lead to an encounter with the transcendent and deeper spiritual experience.

I consider sensitiveness to be an important concept because it is a quality of being that allows us to be attuned to the spirituality that exists in everyday life and all traditions.

Sensitiveness enables us to find the spirit wherever we are. You don't have to go looking for it "out there." The capacity for mystical experience is always present in our lives as long as we cultivate sensitiveness, and this is one of the aims of spiritual practice.

The Experience of Love

At the center of this experience is knowing love—God's love and the power of love—is the outcome of a mystical experience. The writer Anne Spencer Thurman, Howard's daughter, concurs in her book *For the Inward Journey*, saying that "The reality which transcends thought must be described in terms of the highest and best we know." The practice of spiritual disciplines, as we will see in the next section, opens us up to the capacity for sensitiveness to the highest.

The primary purpose for the experience of love, or sensitiveness, is to allow the mystic (or person of strong faith) to "have an intrinsic interest in another person." I understand Anne Spencer Thurman to be saying that this is a universal possibility. Still, this is no ordinary love, where we love for the sake of loving or to feel warm and fuzzy. Love borne of mystical experience is distinctive because it calls us to look beyond ourselves, beyond our personal needs and interests, to another person, not for who she is at any point in time or at any thing she has done, but at the person in her *fact*, or her entirety. We discover that "a person's fact includes more than his plight, predicament, or need at a particular moment in time. It is something total which includes [our] awareness of the person's potential."

Love, therefore, is the act of extending one's concern to the totality of another in the context of the person's whole life and being, to meet the needs of the other as they define those needs.

Love is a giving of one's self for another's sake. By seeing others as we see ourselves, we open ourselves to the other's personality and personhood. This outward expression of love needs "to be worked at, cultivated as a kind of inner development." It is here that we uncover, quite subtly, the core of all spiritual discipline.

Love is an ongoing spiritual discipline, according to Thurman in *Disciplines of the Spirit*. It requires continual effort and extending one's self to others, using "a sensitive and structured imagination." While one might naturally assume the term "imagination" is a psychological term, in Thurman's vision, imagination speaks directly to something that is deeply theological. The imagination enables us to act as *angelos*, messengers of the Holy, by putting ourselves in another's place empathetically, without judgment or prejudice, and using such knowledge to share one's deepest inner resources. By "sitting where they sit," we avoid the taint of selfishness (that is, focusing only on our own needs *and affairs), so we can fill the need of the other exactly as the other requires it. This is what redemption* means.

Meeting the needs of others at their moment of deepest need and seeing them as they see themselves when they are at their best enables us to become divine instruments: We become the instruments of divine love capable of carrying that love to the rest of the world.

When I fully grasp this notion of love, I am compelled to view my beloved through a different lens. I look at her not for what she or our relationship can do for me, but what I can do for her or our relationship. In other words, I live out my relationship with my wife by giving of myself for the explicit purpose of helping her grow spiritually. I confess that I have grown to take this conception of love quite seriously in my marriage. I've also used this understanding of pastoral counseling with individuals and couples in both pre-marital and marriage counseling because it serves as a litmus test for behavior within a loving relationship.

Like any spiritual discipline, love requires an enormous amount of practice. You don't just say that you're going to be this way and you're suddenly transposed into a new, loving creature. You take it step-by-step with continual reinforcement, reflection, and tweaking.

Here is an example: My wife and I were out fishing together on a cold, wintry, but sunny afternoon. We both love to fish even if we don't catch anything. As we were on the riverbank casting our lines, mine got caught in a tree branch that I'd tried carefully not to snag. Attempting to untangle my fishing line, my wife began teasing me and insisting that she could get it loose faster. Being a fairly serious and determined person, I initially refused her assistance. As she kept talking, I could feel my ire arising within my body. My instinct was to lash out and say something harsh like, "Shut up." But I love my wife deeply and I knew that she was having fun in the moment and had no ill intention toward me. At that moment, I thought about what would help us continue having a fun day together and would allow her to be her jovial self without restraint or feeling intimidated by my anger. So, with a fair amount of self-control, I resisted the urge to respond in a negative, hurtful way. In essence, I self-soothed myself and looked into her beautiful, smiling face and handed her the rod so she could try to untangle the line. We ended up cutting the line, tying on more tackle, and moving to another spot. In the end, I felt closer to my wife. There was more love between us, and I knew within me that I had grown in my spiritual practice of love.

As you read this, I hope you grasp that the concept of love presented here is not a sentimental endeavor; it is a lifelong pursuit. As I reflect upon it myself, I immediately see why some of my early attempts at love (of God, other persons, and self) have not quite measured up. I would quickly admit that it was no fault of my own, my parents, or my community. This sort of understanding of love is not something taught in most religious or spiritual communities. We hear some version of it, but seldom with this degree of impact or depth. I confess that I came to my understanding of love through trial and error, reading about many experiences of love, and putting those into practice. Because of my search and struggle for love, and to know what love is or might be in its truest form, when I encountered this framework for love, it immediately made sense to me.

This meaning-making and resonance are specific benefits of dwelling with the mystic, who can bring it alive and help take us to a deeper place in our own lives. Moreover, this concept of love takes time to grasp and live out. Then, with complete honesty, we can look at our own lives, confront ourselves, and correct the errors of our ways. I say this not from a place of high-minded righteousness, but from a place of humility and a desire to help us all grow in the life of faith.

Chapter 17

Love and Social Justice

Love in its mystical form has consequences for those on the frontlines of social justice. We live out the love ethic as we extend ourselves to others, regardless of race, religion, sexual orientation, or culture. Restricting ourselves to these categories dampens the spirit of free-flowing love. Therefore, all structures in society that prevent loving communion between persons are unjust. According to Thurman,

> "Then it is clear that any structure of society, any arrangements under which human beings live that does not provide for maximum opportunities for free-flowing and circulation among each other, works against individual and social health. Any attitudes, private or social, which prohibit people from coming into 'across the board' contact with each other work against the love ethic. It doesn't matter how meaningful it may be the tight circle of isolated security in which individuals or groups move. The existence of such circles precludes the possibility of the experiences of love as a part of intentional living."

Here he interjects the commandment to love one's enemies. It is clear that love precludes our natural or instinctive inclinations; it requires acting at a level of "deliberate intent." By baring our inner selves to others at the core of their being and digging beyond the visible aspects to seek others' inmost selves.

We become better capable of dealing with persons in their totality, wholesomely and redemptive. This form of love is selfless, kind, gentle, accepting, forgetting transgressions, and unrelenting. To accomplish this, we keep the door to our hearts open so that love "gets through...at [the other's] center."

Bringing his view of the love ethic full circle, Thurman insisted that this is how eternal love responds to humans. We experience that love amid our human iniquity. Thurman says, "To love, is the most profound act of religious faith. It is an act that continually renews itself. It is an act that faith exemplars must intentionally perpetuate. You cannot have a mystical experience of love unless you are willing to offer this type of love. Responding with love is the worthiest act of gratitude that you can offer to the universe, the source of love in its most authentic form.

I've witnessed such outpourings of love in congregations, in the workplace, and especially in the family. Consider the brother that gives us a kidney for another family member or friend. Consider the parent who puts his or her career on indefinite hold while their child goes to school just so they can spend quality time together every day after the child comes home. Consider the love and sense of duty of a military member who takes a bullet or grenade for his fellow unit members. Consider the mother whose child was bullied and committed suicide, who is moved to work to change local, state, and federal laws so that other people's children can attend school with legal protection from bullying. Each of these is fueled by a love "that passes all understanding." Each is an example of a person called to look beyond the self in loving service to others.

SECTION IV

THE SPIRITUAL PRACTICES

Chapter 18

Understanding the Importance of Spiritual Practices

Years ago, when I heard the phrase "spiritual practices," I immediately conjured up images of people chanting or walking the labyrinth in search of ultimate truth. Or I pictured a person sitting in the lotus position, quiet and meditating with a clear or blank mind. The word *discipline*, when attached to the word *spiritual*, suggested to me a life of minimal comfort and pleasure, far removed from everyday niceties, with a heavy dose of physical pain to make it last. I've grown to understand that spiritual practices, used synonymously with spiritual disciplines, need not be harsh to be meaningful and life-affirming. Incorporating activities into your life that deepen your spiritual experience can be as simple as increasing your awareness at any given moment.

Here we define spiritual practice as *any activity that you intentionally avail yourself of for the express purpose of awakening yourself to the fullness of life and your relationship to the sacred.* This definition is intentionally broad, so even the simplest and the most complex activities might be experienced as a spiritual practice. I want to demystify spiritual practices as "traveling the road to becoming a person of deep faith," or to demystify the process of becoming a mystic!

Becoming Your Best You

The reason I encourage practice is so that you can grow into becoming the true you, holistically. The true you is the person who learns to master life on the spiritual level, and who is confident in their own skin as a human spirit, no matter which path they've chosen. Spiritual practices promote unity from within by helping you feel anchored to yourself. Imagine a tall building or skyscraper jutting up into the sky. Such a structure cannot stand without a strong foundation. That foundation must have a deep supporting structure below the ground, otherwise, it will topple over from its weight or the wind. Engaging in spiritual practices is a way of developing a firm foundation within yourself. The more you practice, the more mastery you achieve.

Hinduism speaks of a *true you*, by acknowledging an enduring self that undergirds the shifting changing self. You can build up the enduring self by practicing yoga, for example. Meditation and reflection will over prolonged periods strengthen the mind, body, and eventually, the personality. In this manner, one begins to identify the inner self, or the enduring self as the foundation or the true self, even as the outer self that others see goes through changes.

Your best self will arise as you grow in spirit and in relationships with yourself, others, and the community; finding deep meaning in your life; and growing in confidence about your purpose, personal mission, or vocation. As each of these becomes more integrated into your life, I can assure you you'll begin to experience life more fully.

Perhaps you are considering spiritual practices to fulfill a desire to connect with the divine. This is a universal human yearning. For me, when this happens, I sense deep gratitude for my ongoing discipline at this stage of my life. I subscribe to a practice of mindfulness because it helps me remain ready when the divine shows up. I've developed the habit of training myself to steady my attention on music at certain times of the day. Since I live close to the forest, I make it a practice to concentrate on the instrumental music I hear as I drive through the forest. As I concentrate, I block out all other distractions. Practicing day after day after day has helped me call upon my powers of concentration when I need it. As a result, I can be ready to focus when a situation demands it.

I can hardly say too much about readiness to encounter the divine when it shows up in my life. As an Air Force chaplain, readiness is always on my mind. Military members have to be ready to deploy, to fight, and to respond when the need arises (to the emergency, crisis, or critical situation). In fact, I keep two bags packed and ready to go at a moment's notice. After all, when the call arrives, it is not the time to begin to get ready. One bag has the indispensable gear that enables me to survive downrange in the event of a chemical attack. The other bag has the necessary uniforms and toiletries that I'd take with me on the road. Both are essential in the midst of deployment and having them at hand indicates readiness. The same thing goes for your spiritual life.

A crisis is not the time to begin engaging in your spiritual practices. You want to begin your spiritual readiness when things are calm providing the necessary time to develop your growing edge.

To experience an encounter with the transcendent forces of the universe, we need to be equally prepared and ready to go. The spiritual disciplines described in this next section will ready your mind, body, and spirit for the ultimate encounter with the spirit of life. To be honest, spiritual disciplines may not necessarily prepare you for optimal physical (body) conditioning, but they can assist you as you go through your fitness routine. For example, I work out daily in the gym. Over time, working out has become a prayer of sorts for me. I don't necessarily have to pray as I go through my routine, but the discipline of retreating to the gym regularly is a prayer in and of itself. You might say that my gym routine is a form of devotion. It is my ode to life and living. I am saying "Yes!" to life and all that it has to offer me by taking care of my physical well-being so that I can be awake and fit to encounter the divine when it appears before me.

You may not find yourself going to the gym regularly as many do. Don't let it worry you. Perhaps you are a gardener, hiker, walker, biker, swimmer, or have some other passion that gets your blood flowing and your heart rate elevated. Whatever it may be, I invite you to view your passion as a part of your spiritual fitness. See it as a way of boosting and supplementing your mind and spirit. By reclassifying your activity, you are readying yourself for the encounter you dream about.

Steady Practice Does It

I believe that the need to nurture your inner life continues throughout your life, regardless of your ability to experience the sacred. What is not nurtured can wither away. My wife is an expert gardener. Last year she grew beautiful plants and flowers in flower boxes in front of our house. Since there is a box right outside my home office window, I could see the colors radiate as I sat at my computer to work and write. I was thoroughly enjoying the blooms and color during the spring months. What I loved was watching the hummingbirds appear to pollinate the flowers. My pleasure came to a slow end after we took a vacation during the summer and there was no one around to water the flowers. They began to fade, then dry up, and later were gone beyond regeneration. Before I knew it, the hummingbirds had stopped gracing our home searching for the sweet nectar. My sadness at the loss of the flowers lasted the rest of the summer. Their absence was a constant reminder of the need for adequate provisions.

The spiritual life is similar. We need to water the soil of our spirit with regularity if it is to flourish and attract nature's wonders. If we develop the habit of caring for our inner lives, the habit becomes less of a burden and more of a pleasure—a necessary part of our lifestyle. Until now, you may not have thought of your spiritual growth as a lifestyle choice, but it is. Like growing flowers in flower boxes, gardening is part of my wife's lifestyle. She does it naturally because it is a part of who she is. She is a gardener. As such, we are all gardeners of our faith. We must work the soil season after season.

Spiritual Practices Help During the Difficult Times

In Unitarian Universalism, we tend to focus on the good in life, creating a form of paradise here on earth. For the majority of people in the world, however, this life on earth is no paradise. It's a jungle out there. Real-life is about mastering difficulties, or as Thurman called them, the "Vicissitudes of life." Just making it from day-to-day can be a struggle. Strong, reliable faith that is grounded in spiritual practices can serve as a shield against hard times. Your faith can be a buffer softening the blow of difficult events in your life. Think of it this way: if you were a gymnast performing a routine on a pommel horse and you fell, you'd rather fall on a rubberized surface than a bare, hard floor. The soft surface would be more likely to prevent a serious injury than a hard one. Your spiritual practices will give you a soft surface to fall upon when difficult times come. And, believe me, they will come, because life is an incubator for solving problems.

The story of Dr. Victor Frankl illustrates this well. The Austrian psychiatrist was captured by the Nazis and held as a prisoner during World War II. While in prison, Dr. Frankl became aware of the prison guards' control over his life and the lives of the other prisoners. Every element of their existence, from waking to sleeping and everything in between had been monitored and controlled by the guards. But the one thing the guards could not control was the prisoners' mindset and the meaning they made of that horrible experience. By realizing that, Dr. Frankl developed personal meditative practices that helped him endure and thrive during his concentration camp experience.

On one occasion he described in his book, *Man's Search for Meaning*, he and his comrades were being marched in the bitter, icy cold by guards who were pushing them with the butts of their rifles. Another prisoner whispered to him, "If our wives could see us now!" That brought images and memories of Dr. Frankl's wife to his mind, and he began a private conversation in his mind with her that led to a vision of her, "more luminous than the sun which was beginning to rise." From that experience, Dr. Frankl realized the true power of love "as the salvation of man," meaning that his deep emotional connection to his wife—his love for her—was an example of the power of love to sustain a person during extreme hardship. His ability to allow love to infuse his inner life became part of his spiritual practice. He wrote, "This intensification of inner life helped the prisoner find a refuge from the emptiness, desolation, and spiritual poverty of his existence..."

This point cannot be overemphasized. Indeed, most of the world's religions, and therefore, religious and spiritual practices, came about in response to big human questions:

Why do we suffer?

How do we contend with the problems of this world?

Why do we have to die?

And perhaps, most important of all, what does this suffering mean?

The latter is the question we often ask ourselves when encountering life's thorns. The word *suffering* tends to be favored by theologians. In reality, when we acknowledge that life is full of troubles, we are, indeed, acknowledging that life is full of suffering. For me, problems and suffering are synonymous because problems bring with them a degree of agony, distress, and misery. And often, our instinctive response to a problem is avoidance or hoping it goes away. Through introspection and grounding yourself, you will be more capable of accepting and facing your problems as they arise.

The grounding that you gain from spiritual practices helps you endure, and indeed, helps you develop resilience so you can bounce back after resolving problems in your life.

One of my rudest awakenings came during my Air Force deployment to Iraq. As a chaplain in the theater hospital, I encountered more challenges dealing with the other chaplains than I did anywhere else. This will surprise those who experience chaplains as universally friendly and representatives of the Holy. While all Protestant chaplains wear the same badge, and cross, in a given military unit the various chaplains come from different denominations. These denominations represent various theological traditions, beliefs, doctrine, rituals, and styles of worship, to name a few. Due to these differences, some chaplains will not work with others, or at least, are often skeptical of one another in ways that affect the cohesiveness of the ministry. This skepticism sometimes comes through in personal and professional interactions.

During my deployment, I found myself in frequent conflict with another chaplain. I was the senior chaplain due to my clinical experience and rank. We worked on opposite shifts at the hospital—me during the day and her at night. It was no secret that she had joined the unit thinking she'd be senior. She was also from a more conservative denomination than mine, as I am endorsed by the Unitarian Universalist Association. While I cannot be certain that was the reason, our differences often resulted in a less-than-collegial relationship, which often made my experience in Iraq frustrating. As an example, when I assumed part of her coverage of a flight line squadron, she refused to give me a thorough tour of the forces and introduce me to important leaders. There was nothing she would allow me to do that didn't start with an argument. Rather than working as a team, we seemed to be adversaries.

When I raised the issue to our superiors, they insisted that they'd address the issue with her. On one occasion, she and I met together with our supervisor to discuss our working relationship. While we agreed in the office, our pattern soon resumed its ugliness back in the unit. I felt as though my hands were tied, a poor position for a military officer. One of my spiritual practices was to debrief weekly with another chaplain to exchange different views on our significant experiences, both spiritual and professional. It was a way of refreshing my spirit in a safe space with a trusted colleague. Through these meetings, I discovered that my hospital colleague was difficult with other chaplains, also. Others had struggled to partner with her and experienced her as occasionally unreliable and less than professional. I realized then that despite my best attempts to make a difficult situation more bearable, my only option was endurance. The only way out of that scenario, other than avoiding her (which wasn't possible), was to wait it out. She would eventually be re-deployed, and I'd gain another chaplain colleague on the night shift. Hopefully, one more collegial. After two or three difficult months, that is exactly what happened. I attribute my ability to overcome that challenging period to my spiritual discipline.

Of course, the whole time I worked with her wasn't terrible. There were many enjoyable aspects to the work beyond the challenges described above. I loved meeting with patients, staff, and the commanders at the hospital day in and day out. I felt respected by the people I've served—partly because of my role and rank—but also due to my personality and demeanor. Like Dr. Frankl, feeling the love of people important to me helped me find sunshine and light when my colleague seemed a source of darkness. The primary reason I was deployed in Iraq was to serve in the hospital, yet that relationship was distasteful to me daily, so I had to find a way to persevere and get through it.

Problems don't always last, as the sacred texts tell us, especially if we learn how to short-circuit or avoid problems. To the extent that we commit ourselves to the right action, abide by the strictures of society, and live by our moral values, we are doing the best we can. The problems we encounter then are likely to be unavoidable. I want to be clear here that I recognize that many people in our world, including in the United States, truly live with their backs against the wall. No amount of right living is going to immunize them from difficult living. This includes large segments of society who are people of color, not heterosexual, immigrants, and other marginalized categories. Ongoing spiritual practice can help us to better cope with these realities and give us a sense of control and confidence that we can manage our struggles rather than surrendering to hopelessness.

Faith Makes You Stronger

Most people look to their faith to become more resilient. I believe that in the aftermath of great struggles, your faith can make you stronger. Such a state is called *antifragile*, a term coined by Professor Nassim Nicholas Taleb. In his text, *Antifragility*, he highlights the differences between the states of being antifragile and resilient. Something antifragile "Is beyond resilience or robustness. The resilient resists shocks and stays the same; the antifragile gets better." Faith, especially exemplary faith, builds the capacity within you to be antifragile. This is great news. Moreover, it ought to give us the incentive to deal with our problems head-on instead of running from them. Using Taleb's theory, we can embrace life's vicissitudes because we know they make us stronger. In doing so, our faith also becomes antifragile.

I believe that much of the unhappiness we encounter in the world is a consequence of our faulty expectations. We grow up with the notion that we should be happy all the time. Nothing can be further from the truth. No one "promised us a rose garden." Then, as we are initiated into the life of faith, we bring this faulty working assumption with us. It becomes a burden on our faith, a sort of litmus test for whether we are sufficiently trusting of God, the spirit of life, or the goodness of people. When things don't go our way, we lean more heavily on our faith to turn things around: "If I trust more, things will get better, God will make it better." If things don't get better over time, our faith continues to take a beating. We end up going to church, synagogue, or mosque week after week to shore up our faith, looking for a solution that never really comes. The solution lies within us, in antifragile faith.

By adjusting our expectations, we can turn around much of our unhappiness. The adjustment is to begin expecting that life will present us with a steady stream of problems to solve. Our job as people of faith is to be ready to encounter these vicissitudes and struggles with courage and fortitude, knowing that we can get through them. We might not come out unscathed, but that is not the aim. From a faith perspective, the bumps and bruises make us antifragile. Just as a bone that heals from a fracture comes back stronger, so does our faith.

Our faith eventually builds muscle memory.

It helps us to remember that we've dealt with a problem before and got through it, so we can get through it again. Eventually, our faith becomes a constant reminder that we can face life's challenges with courage and strength. We welcome the challenges because we know they make us stronger—antifragile.

Faith as a Prophylaxis

As our faith becomes antifragile, we develop a spiritual and psychological "hedge of protection" from life's vicissitudes that inevitably arrive. This is the essence of mastering your faith. If you imagine the hedges around your home that separate your yard from your neighbor's, you realize that the protection of the hedges is not that of a brick wall, but it will prevent some things, like a large ball or even an animal, from crossing into your yard. Surely, the animal could go around the hedge, but at least the hedge slows down most incursions into your property. Hedges also provide a little privacy. In the same manner, faith operates as a semi-permeable barrier to some parts of life where you'd prefer some protection. As we said earlier, faith does not prevent hard times, but it affords you a layer of security that helps you maintain yourself and endure. It preserves your spiritual integrity.

I believe that faith exemplars have this type of faith. Not only are they antifragile, but they also have an invisible security blanket with them daily. When tough times pass, these exemplars look largely unchanged. They know their faith brought them through. It is the same for the humanist. She knows that she'll get through life's storms because her trust in self is the true shelter. Although an umbrella will not stop the rain, it will keep you dry and allow you to walk through the rain without getting soaking wet. You might get some moisture on your clothes, water on your shoes, and a little mist in your face, but all-in-all, you will be intact. If you use it, faith can provide the same kind of protection. Over time, you'll be antifragile, too.

Chapter 19

Commitment

There is no better place to start with spiritual disciplines than with *commitment*. When we commit ourselves to anything, we promise or make a covenant with ourselves that we will do it. Commitment is the firm foundation of strong faith. As Thurman says, *"Commitment is a self-conscious act of the will by which [you] affirm [your] identification with what [you are] [devoted] to."* This is where the intention is born, within the consciousness of your mind, on your own volition. Deep within the recesses of your being lives a dormant source of power that you can use to firmly seed your faith. Once we align our consciousness with the promise we undertake, our sense of commitment becomes a reality. That is all commitment is— getting our intention lined up with our actions, then following through with effort.

When you look back on your life, you'll probably find that commitment generates spiritual energy. It's as if a fire had been ignited within you and a source of energy turned on. This process takes place any time you have a new goal that you're committed to accomplishing. Goals focus our attention. The clearer the goal, the more concentrated your energy. Commitment has the same potential, but we must learn to harness the power and aim it in the right direction. Thurman insists that when we are "Able to bring to bear upon a single purpose all the powers of our being, our whole life is energized and vitalized."

If you want to see this in real-time, just show up at a gym during January. The place will be packed with people who are energized to meet their New Year commitments. Show up a month later and you'll discover who is committed. Usually, the place is a lot less crowded and less energized because the level of commitment has faded away for the majority of exercisers. The trick is to keep up your level of commitment by maintaining your consciousness, energy, focus, and effort. Don't allow yourself to drop out of pursuing your spiritual goals and objectives. Treat your spiritual life with the same level of commitment that you maintain for your work life or your family life. Your wellbeing depends on it.

The Sure Foundation

I hope it is becoming clear that spiritual commitment is the foundation for all other spiritual disciplines; it establishes the degree and depth of how we practice our devotional life. Viewing commitment as a practice solidifies your grounding. If you can commit to commitment, you can commit to anything that you put your mind to. Still, we are human. If you find yourself lacking the willpower to pull this off, Thurman encourages you, saying, "Every effort must be put forth to find out what the hindrance is. No exception is permissible." This may seem like an extreme statement, yet it is necessary.

Search yourself and find out what are your barriers and distractions are and remove them. That means eradicating all barriers to your goals. When we do this, something inside of us says, "Yes."

I realize that this "just do it" type of language may sound *passé*, or even flip, especially to freethinkers and others from liberal traditions. In reality, creating this foundation for your faith has less to do with any tradition than with opening up one's mind and heart to a new way of understanding the self.

Commitment is about setting aside the ego, that part of you that wants to do things your way and your way only.

When you put the ego aside, you are freed to allow other possibilities to take root in your being. Act as if what you are being called to do is the truth. Put aside your identifiers or status that might prevent you from gaining new insight and power from within yourself. In other words, you can decide to put yourself into a state of deep cooperation with this new view of yourself as a person of deep commitment. Therefore being more sincere and honest cooperating with yourself (and others). Once you do, you'll find that commitment extends beyond yourself as an individual.

Let's go a little deeper into this idea of commitment. We can say in more theological terms that commitment is a supreme claim upon us, by God, the universe, or an ultimate reality, for a cause or purpose beyond the self. In this case, that cause, or purpose is to grow in faith and serve in love. Yielding to this claim upon ourselves and our lives is the essence of commitment.

Chapter 20

Growing in wisdom and stature

Being able to experience growth is an important aspect of the spiritual journey. If you're on any type of journey, even for a few feet or yards, you want the sensation that you're moving in the right direction, working your way toward a goal. Growth is so important because if you're being interviewed for a job, the interviewer will ask upfront what your personal goals are and how you'd plan on growing with the company. It seems natural that growth in our spiritual life is what we want to achieve. But what does growth in wisdom and character mean?

For our purposes, growth refers to a process by which a person moves along a continuum that begins at a fundamental state and develops into an increasingly mature and exemplary capacity for faith. A person may enter this continuum at any point along the way, going forward or back, or inching along as life experience dictates. The most basic illustration is a seed growing into a mature plant. If properly nurtured, the seed will grow until it reaches full maturity. However, as circumstances change, and as the seed grows, it may encounter seasonal adjustments and conditions that are out of the ordinary, and its growth cycle will adapt. If the soil becomes overly dry, growth is likely to falter. If there is too much sunshine or heat, the plant may wilt. If the garden is neglected, it may be overtaken by weeds or insects. Therefore, the plant's owner must be mindful and attend to a variety of factors to assure the plant's growth. Our faith development is the same, with one exception. We are both the seed and the gardener. We have to faithfully tend to all of the variables that affect our inner lives. If we do, our faith grows and our roots go deeper. Without proper attention, we will not grow.

Changes to Structure and Quality of Character

The specific growth that Thurman had in mind when he spoke about wisdom and stature referred to "A change in structure and quality of character." This means undergoing some fundamental positive shifts in your personality and spiritual makeup, where you become something more than who you were at the beginning of your faith journey. For example, by participating in a meditative spiritual practice, you may find your heart more open to giving and being generous with your time and other resources. By reading sacred scriptures or spiritual books, you may become more compassionate to homeless people or those without jobs. These are both structural and quality of life changes, altering your priorities and activities to sustain and enhance your spiritual nature.

A personal example might be helpful here. Generally, I've been a thrifty person, saving funds from a young age, and learning the value of money. I had bank accounts as a kid and later deposited some savings with every paycheck. Likewise, I learned early on about the spiritual obligation of giving away part of my money to help others, primarily by donating to my church. I felt obliged to give as I'd followed my mother's example, and various spiritual commandments related to generosity. In the last decade of my life, I've learned to shift my attitudes and my perspectives on giving by listening to the financial strategist, advisor, and life coach, Dave Ramsey. He teaches the value of being debt-free and maintaining integrity in one's life about giving. I learned to give (not out of necessity or obligation) but because giving is a virtue and a worthwhile spiritual goal. Intentionally working on being generous is a spiritual challenge for me because something inside craves to hold on to the money! It's true. An old fear of scarcity within me pushes up against my desire to change, tempting me to fall into old patterns. In some circumstances, I need to remind myself that I don't need to listen to my old self, preferring to live by my new values.

I strive now to donate to people and causes, as the benefits I derive are spiritual. This helps me to experience my soul growing and my heart expanding. I'm less concerned about having more money tucked away. My systematic method of saving and investing remains integral to my financial goals, but now my strategies have an important faith element that helps keep me in check. Now, I can save and give with more spiritual consciousness. And I can honestly say that I feel more integrity in my talk and my walk. Giving doesn't have to be limited to monetary resources. Being vigilant for opportunities to give my time and experience to various causes is equally gratifying. At the heart of these structural and character shifts is an internal sense that you are aligning your deep convictions with your everyday actions. As you are practicing what you preach, you grow in wisdom and stature.

Growth and the Seasonal Nature of Change

Growth is a process of enduring the seasons of becoming who you are. No one grows from seedling to a full-grown tree overnight. Many seasons pass along the path of growing up and maturing in faith. Not only do the seasons of the year pass, our seasons of faith pass as well. For me, like many religious persons, a season is a part of my life that is in flux. There are many seasons, not just those on the calendar. Writing this book, for example, marks a season of generativity. I'm feeling creative in my spiritual life as I write out this manuscript.

There have been seasons when I've felt strong and seasons when I've felt sickly. A sickly season may have been a period when I've caught a cold or found myself in the doctor's office more than usual. During that period, which may have lasted for a few weeks or months, I'd say to myself that I was in a season of illness. Similarly, at the beginning of almost every decade of my life, I've felt my body going through some type of metamorphosis. As I was going through one of these periods, I've always known that it would eventually end. Having that self-assurance, based on my life history, I was able to bear it more patiently. I also knew that I probably hadn't done anything wrong in my lifestyle, it was a period of change in my physical body. In every instance, I'd come through feeling well and with my sense of self intact, physically, emotionally, and spiritually.

Growing in stature and wisdom is the same thing. Sometimes, you'll find you're on your A-game, other times, you're not. It's a process. You're a seasonal creature. It's important to note this process of seasonal development to maintain realistic expectations for yourself as you grow. The more you expect the seasons, there are fewer chances of feeling less productive, non-spiritual, and melancholy. Adjusting your expectations should strengthen your discipline helping you to keep up with your practice. To paraphrase scriptural language, darkness lasts for a night, but joy comes in the morning. During some seasons, it will feel like everything is in darkness, but you know that warmth, light, and sunshine shall rise. You will grow over time. Remember that it is a process.

Regarding the seasonality of growth, recognize that you can only grow to the extent that you are able and ready at the time. Who among us hasn't wanted to move to the next level of a career or responsibility before it was time? Were we super-anxious about moving up, overconfident about our ability to do our boss's job, or simply impatient? We usually can't move up just based on desire alone; we also need the skills and know-how. Personal seasons change as our capacity to evolve develops. This is a fact of true faith that we need to learn to master. As your capacity increases, so does your growth in stature and wisdom. With that you can grasp the concept of personal growth and recognize the real-life change as it occurs is the sign that you are indeed growing in your faith.

Dealing With Crisis

Crises test your stature and form. When your everyday approach of handling business is disrupted, how you respond gives you immediate feedback about your competence as a person of faith and your capacity to generate and rely on wisdom. The crisis here is not an emergency, those developmental crises that appear are forks in the road of life. Which way do you go? Which path do you choose? Or better yet, as Thurman put it in *With Head and Heart*, how do you resolve "The tension between the impulse to go forward and the impulse to stay put?" As long as the two impulses stand in opposition to one another, there is tension. Such tension is unsustainable over time. Growth occurs when one impulse claims victory over the other. Even if you appear to be at a stalemate with a decision and decide not to act (some may say that they are unable to decide). As soon as you become aware that a decision is needed, you will have a new basis for going forward, and the old basis for indecision will fade away.

I had a pastoral counseling client who could not decide whom to marry. Between two women in his life, he couldn't figure out which one he was the most compatible with. He loved them both. After some time, he deliberated intensely without ever deciding for one or the other. This was a personal crisis for him. Even though he was unable to decide—a painful psychological state, I admit—his awareness of the decision point in itself changed the basis, or foundation, of future decisions. For example, he could not claim a lack of awareness as a basis for not deciding, and thereby, liberate himself from the crisis. Personal awareness eliminates ignorance as an excuse. Failure or refusal to decide does not mean you're not growing. It may mean a fear of growing or moving out of one's comfort zone. From a pastoral counseling perspective, it could be viewed as choosing to stunt personal growth and remain in an impoverished state of development. To the extent that committing points to a healthier state of spiritual affairs, then not making a decision points in the opposite direction. Both committing or not committing would relieve the tension of the crisis and reveal something about this client's capacity for growth in spiritual discipline.

As Thurman reminds us in *Disciplines*, "All our life long we are fashioning a private pattern made up of the resolutions of the crises of growth. Such a pattern gives to each life a dominant trend which becomes an essential—not a casual—part of character." Maybe this was an indication he needed not to make a decision. Perhaps, neither woman was right? Or, he needed more time before he decided? These are questions of faith that I could not answer. However, I can encourage you to choose life, choose growth, and realize your faith's full potential.

Chapter 21

Suffering

Virtually every spiritual and religious tradition addresses suffering as an inevitable part of life. It is a universal condition of human existence no matter how much money we have, how often we exercise or pay attention to our well-being, how much we pray or meditate, or try to avoid this reality. In *Disciplines of the Spirit*, Howard Thurman defines one kind of suffering as "Physical pain or its equivalent, about which the individual may be inspired to protect himself, so that despite its effects he may carry on the functioning of his life." I would add to this emotional, psychic, and spiritual pain. All of these aspects contribute to the suffering in our lives. The experience of suffering can serve as a spiritual discipline, helping us to cope better with life's changes. People with strong faith understand that in life, "rain falls on the good and the bad;" no one is exempt. Recognizing this can help us embrace suffering in ways that move us forward toward our personal, vocational, and spiritual goals.

I've discovered that the shortcut to managing suffering is acceptance. Buddhism considers acceptance as the key to alleviate suffering. By accepting the reality that we are born into suffering, that is—to encounter problems in our lives—we put to rest the idea that life should be pain-free, worry-free, and full of happiness, and that if we are not experiencing perpetual happiness something is dreadfully wrong in our lives. Or worse yet, that something is wrong with us as individuals. When we accept that life is an incubator for confronting and resolving problems to be continually faced head-on, then the fact of suffering loses its power over us, and we can take our power back. In the meantime, we need a framework for working through suffering and use it for growth.

Inventory Personal Resources

As a spiritual discipline, pain can lead the sufferer to take inventory of personal resources available for dealing with problems head-on. My most valuable resource when I find myself struggling is my network of personal relationships. I turn to my wife, Tamara, first and foremost, for conversation and perspective. Having her as a confidant and friend creates a safe place to begin working myself out of a difficult situation. Because her background and experience differ from mine, I can count on her to open my eyes to the reality I am confronting and view it from a different angle. If you have a spouse, partner, or significant other that you trust and feel safe with, I encourage you to consider this personal resource before you turn to others outside of your relationship. You may counter this with something like, "My partner doesn't understand blah-blah-blah. It's too complicated." It doesn't matter. She or he knows you and is not you! That improves the chances of gaining a fresh perspective. Equally important, by trusting your partner to lend her or his valuable perspective, you build trust and faith in your primary relationship, assuming the relationship is in a good place and is supportive.

The next resource that I consider is people in my personal and professional networks, depending on what type of problem I am trying to reflect on and resolve. This broader circle includes close friends and work colleagues. I turn to them for understanding, compassion, and expertise. Ninety-nine percent of the time what I experience is not new. But, hearing from others who love and care for me helps me struggle along more gracefully without feeling alone in my situation. The blessing of hearing others' wisdom is priceless. Thurman says it this way in *Disciplines*: "Through the ministry of [your] own burden," you may be drawn into a community with other sufferers to find solutions. Yet, the real mark of wisdom flows from your capacity to implement the suggestions of others. People can talk to you until they are blue in the face, but if you aren't willing to put those suggestions into action, their experience goes for naught. It takes real faith to act.

In my parish work, I frequently encounter people who tell me they are unable to speak publicly about their private lives. This may be a result of shyness or a lack of close friendships. My professional and pastoral response is to encourage them to seek out a support group, a clergy person, or professional counseling. Support groups of similarly situated persons offer safe environments for opening up at your speed, or sometimes, not at all. Group members will let you simply listen and find someone whom you have chemistry with during social time. You can also find helpful professionals through most health insurance plans. For those without insurance or employee benefits for mental health, it may require some creativity, but local social service agencies can be of help as well.

The Power of Vulnerability to Ease Suffering

There is also much to be gained by making myself vulnerable and visible to others during times of trouble. As C.S. Lewis said in his book, *A Grief Observed*, "[Trying to] conceal the pain increases the burden." I've found that being transparent brings out people who can help me, otherwise they'd never have known I needed assistance. Once people hear my story, they are empowered to walk alongside me during my time of need. In essence, I permit them publicly to come forth to my aid. If I had kept the dilemma to myself, I'd never have heard from those empathic souls. Therefore, being vulnerable before others is a way of making our spiritual discipline of suffering public, not for show, but to open ourselves up to others' love and share in our humanity.

Identity With a Holy and Human Presence

The stories of public suffering by people such as Gandhi or Mother Theresa have helped millions of people cope with their suffering. Gandhi, who was a man of means before the Indian revolution, took up making his clothes to be in solidarity with the poor. Such people who have taken up vows of poverty to suffer with the poor and disenfranchised show us that to suffer is not only a noble act, it can also be a calling, a sacred vocation. They demonstrate to us that there is no shame in suffering. The saints and religious leaders of many traditions have shown us that not only can we survive the unbearable, but also come out stronger and more resilient.

The path of Siddhartha Gautama, the Buddha, as mentioned earlier, is another story that inspires many. What I find intriguing is his teaching of the Middle Way. As one who grew up in extreme wealth and subsequently denounced that lifestyle, he began seeking a holier, more noble path by studying with the Hindu masters of his time. After learning all that he could from them, he sought out the other end of the spectrum by joining the ascetics, deeply religious people who lived under self-imposed austerity. As Houston Smith points out in *The Illustrated World's Religions*, "Living the ascetic life taught Gautama the futility of asceticism" and inspired him to create "the Middle Way between the extremes of asceticism and indulgence." Many of us moderns can relate to the Buddha's spiritual practice of moderation, especially when much of what we encounter in the world encourages extreme approaches to taking care of ourselves. This aspect of the Buddha's approach invites us to consider a middle-of-the-road perspective that still makes room for holiness and the sacred in your life.

If you are a person who does not resonate with religious personalities, you can review the life of a favorite public, non-religious personality who has overcome difficulties and great suffering. You can even look to your own family. I've found incredible strength in my parents, as many have found in theirs. My mother, for example, told me several years ago how she learned to live with various medical conditions and accept that some were a direct result of aging and couldn't be reversed. Upon hearing and reflecting on that, I slowly began to understand how my health was not going to be perfect, and I needed to make peace with a chronic condition (an autoimmune disorder). Over time, I've come to understand that personal suffering is humbling and a constant reminder of human frailty and finitude.

I imagine that if you look among your family and friends, or recall stories that you'd read, you will find fine examples of people who have learned to embrace suffering in its various forms. One such person I encountered was Joel Marc Filmore, a biracial gay man whose mother was murdered by his stepfather when Joel was three years old. He'd experienced racial hatred as a young person, then abuse by his family and hometown natives. He eventually ended up on the streets of Chicago, living, as he said, as a "Homeless, drug-addicted cross-dressing prostitute." Over eleven years, he was arrested fifty-seven times and served eighteen months of a three-year prison sentence.

Joel describes himself as non-religious. Yet, with time on his hands in prison "to do nothing," he read the Bible from cover to cover and connected deeply with the message that he was loved. The message did not convert him to Christianity or any other religion, but it transformed his understanding of himself as someone who could be loved. Sitting there in his cell, his life changed. According to Joel, "Things that held me back my entire life no longer held sway over me. I'm still not a religious person, I don't attend any organized functions, but I believe that my life is guided by the divine, and I honor that." While in prison, he earned a bachelor's degree in psychology and now serves as a core faculty member and staff therapist at the Family Institute at Northwestern University in Chicago. Persons such as Joel Filmore in no manner are giving up, giving in or succumbing to hopelessness. Rather, they model a mature response to the human condition and its imperfections. They are faith exemplars that we may strive to emulate in our own lives.

Chapter 22

Prayer

At the core of many religious and spiritual traditions lies the discipline of prayer. Thurman's definition of prayer is universal in its content and process. In his book, *The Creative Encounter*, he defined prayer as "The method by which the individual makes his way to the temple of quiet within his spirit and the activity of his spirit within its walls." Identifying prayer, in general terms, as a method, grounds it as a means by which we shape our faith. This also leaves the door open to allow us to create and modify our way of doing prayer (or not) that fits with where we are along the spectrum of faith. If you are beginning your journey of faith, there is a place for you. Likewise, if you are a journeyman, a person skilled in prayer life, there is a place for you, too. There is also room for persons to pray who seek communication with the transcendent, but not with a being or deity; those people pray to the Universe. That type of prayer is as much a spiritual discipline as other more traditional forms of prayer.

An In-depth Look Into the Definition of Prayer

Going deeper into our definition of prayer, we might surmise that it is largely an individual and personal practice at its core. For me, the personal aspect is liberating, because we are freed to customize our prayer life and not succumb to others' conception of what is right for us. In Unitarian Universalism, this tends to bring out the creative aspect of the spiritual life. People bring aspects of their whole lives, as well as the lives of others, to the praying moment. Within the Unitarian Universalist worship tradition, the type of prayer one experiences depends on the theological leaning of the congregation and the minister. You are likely to hear a prayer that lifts your spirit and warms your soul, but with a broader theological framework than traditional Protestant offerings. I've found that deeply engaging prayer in such a context expands me, but at the same time, my heart yearns for the familiar prayers of my youth. Yet, I realize that retreating to the prayer practices of earlier days has its shortcomings, too. This points to the realization that our spiritual journey is continually unfolding. Perhaps, for spiritual freethinkers and spiritual liberals, there is no perfect way, only the acceptance that there are many ways to pray, and many paths to the divine. However you should choose to pray is a valid way of practicing this vital spiritual discipline.

The wisdom of Thurman's definition, found in *Disciplines of the Spirit*, is that it allows us to "Make [the] way to the temple of quiet" that lies within us. What can be more healing and transformational than knowing that within each of us lies a quiet space to reflect on the faith that we wish to grow and expand? Linking the ancient description of the body as a temple to our current understanding of prayer rightfully connects our spiritual discipline with those of our spiritual ancestors. Unitarian Universalists trace our faith ancestors back to the first century of Christian practice and doctrine, but we often lose sight of those ancient traditions. This language concerning the temple within us grounds us squarely in our origins, knowing that our faith lives have historical precedents and are not just the latest "thing" or fad. Tradition grounds us in a ritual that has endured throughout the centuries.

The "activity of the spirit" refers to human communication with the divine. Traditionally, this is the goal of prayer—connecting us with the divine presence within so that we might be guided in the ways of truth, love, and compassion. To be known by God, however we define it. Whether your communion with spirit is by spoken prayer, meditation, chanting, singing, or a combination of thereof, truth, love, and compassion remains a central aim of prayer.

Rounding out this definition of prayer, "within its walls" refers to the temple within or human person itself. Each of us is a being of finite boundaries that define us from the world, and these walls serve as a holding environment for our prayers. And yet, being in community with others, we can expand the walls of spirit and form a more extensive and inclusive temple from which to communicate with the divine.

Further Ways of Understanding Prayer

Prayer is the path to communion with God, the means of sharing God's love with others, and the avenue for expressing thanksgiving. This is the core of much religious and spiritual seeking, especially for people of strong faith who desire to commune with the divine, almost as if this impulse is *the* human impulse. I respect this profound search because it reinforces Thurman's notion that at the heart of all spirituality is the desire to be known by God. How else might we be known than by being in communion with the divine presence? Or with the universe? With nature? Each of these is a core expression of making meaning because by being in connection with the ultimate source you invite meaning into your life.

There have been times when I was in a communal worship setting and the space seemed to be filled with the power of love. That power was as palpable as it could be without being in physical form. If the sense of love could have been a mist, it would have covered everyone in the room. That is what *sharing God's love with others* means in the context of prayer. In this respect, praying is a means of acknowledging the divine presence and becoming one with it. So, becoming one with others also engages in the act of prayer. Being in unison with others, focusing your attention, and opening your heart with the same intention is the essence of sharing of spirit or soul. When this is accompanied by touching or holding hands, it might be described as the sharing of body and soul.

In those moments of communal prayer, I have been filled with gratitude—gratitude for being aware of the moment, but also for being able to participate in the moment with others, who often feel similarly touched by grace. Often, when this sensation rolls over me, it feels like a mystical moment.

More often than not, prayer is a practice bringing us "Strength and renewal for our spirits, lest we perish," says Thurman in *Disciplines*. Whether you believe in God, a "higher power," or not—prayer can be the respite you need to regenerate your spirit.

By taking the time to connect with that ultimate source of life, we find a respite for ourselves from the daily grind or those concerns that often weigh heavily upon us. If only for a brief moment, we turn it all over to the great beyond.

That is not to say that we relinquish our responsibility or obligations. Instead, it is a means of sharing our load with the universe by taking a spiritual timeout from the burdens and daily tides of life. Otherwise, the heaviness of life can feel oppressive.

A Word on Prayer for Non-praying People

For those who are not the praying kind, I believe this is an important topic to explore a little further. Being able to relate to or understand those who are different from you, who do pray, can be a bridge to greater faith, bringing respect for others of different beliefs and practices. For those with a devout belief or conviction regarding prayer, it is a source of comfort, lifting one's burdens. It offers psycho-spiritual relief for those who see themselves praying to a transcendent personified source. For them, prayer is both a request for relief and a passing of a burden that weighs heavily on them. Even when illness becomes chronic, prayer serves as a source of solace and consolation, knowing that divine source is journeying alongside you.

I've experienced non-believers and those skeptical of prayer become distressed over prayer because they are convinced that there is no one to pray to, and that invalidates the practice in their eyes. They might ask, what is the purpose of such petitions if no one is out there to answer? This point of view, however, misses the point of the prayer from a faith perspective altogether, because it overlooks or minimizes the trust, hope, and confidence inherent in the act itself. As I conceive of prayer, one does it to exercise one's faith, not to receive an answer, even though one may be just a prayer away. While many do pray for answers and divine benevolence, I don't necessarily advocate looking for such returns.

There is also the discipline of prayer, and the felt response that propels those who are praying into a state of release and spiritual well-being. If you can imagine how it feels to unburden yourself with a close friend or family member with news or of pressing concerns of any kind. Then you'll also recall the sense of relief you've felt at the listener's willingness to sit with you and hear your concern. Therefore, you should be able to empathize with those who pray. This goes both ways. Ideally, those you unburden yourself to can empathize with you.

The important distinction between prayer and a friendly conversation is that prayer has a spiritual intent and content that seeks a soul-growing outcome, and if the praying person desires it, a movement that unites us with the spirit of life, nature, the universe, God, or however you want to see it, often wields transformational results.

Often, as Thurman reminds us, the person praying is seeking that quietude that resides deep within us.

Ultimately, what makes someone a faith exemplar is to recognize that there are many paths to mastering faith. None are superior or subordinate to the others. Each of us has a particular means of reaching and connecting with the spirit of life itself. Someone who recognizes the power of spiritual practice can promote the potential for spiritual evolution, and transcends differences between us for the sake of a loving, more just world.

A Suggestion About Prayer Practices

As the beloved poet Rumi says, "There are a thousand ways to kneel and kiss the ground." That is one way of saying that you can pray in any way that makes sense to you. I'd like to offer you a basic template for how to pray. Feel free to modify it to suit your personal and spiritual needs.

First, you should settle down, be still, and find a quiet place. This will simply put you in a physically relaxed posture. Though you can pray in any posture, being relaxed can facilitate your release of cares and concerns, and your receptivity to receive. Buddhists, Hindus, and others, for example, often pray in a lotus position wearing comfortable clothing, to accommodate contemplation. Muslims and others kneel side-by-side, prostrating themselves. It is totally up to you.

Once in the posture of your choosing, Thurman encourages us to wait for a "Centering moment that will redefine, reshape, and refocus our lives." Sometimes, when I'm offering a congregational prayer, I stand at the pulpit, then wait for that centering moment to find me. In that space, it doesn't take long, a matter of seconds, for the moment to take hold. When I prayed as a child with my grandmother, side-by-side at my bedside, I approached the position already mentally centered. Embedded in Thurman's words of advice is an understanding that we stand ready to be changed by the act of prayer. We expect to be changed and transformed in some form or another. That is what he means by redefine, reshape, and refocus. We bring ourselves to the moment of embracing change.

Then, we pray. The actual act may consist of verbalizing words, thinking of words, listening to others' words, or simply meditating on the sounds heard at the moment. You could, of course, read a prayer or recite one from memory. Your prayer can be as simple as a few words or as complex as a lamentation about the struggles of your life and those you know, or a petition for a deep need in your life. There are no limits, but that you try to go at it from a place of sincerity and offer a genuine outpouring of your heart and soul.

My most common prayer arises from the feeling of closeness that I get from spending time with my wife. The most dominant feelings are joy, happiness, and gratitude. I'm happy to be with her, enjoying the relationship that we've created and worked on together, relishing the partnership we practice as a couple. Perhaps, previous experience of marriage shapes my understanding of how difficult marriage can be. When a relationship works out the way you hope for, your prayer seems to be answered. That, for me, is reason to say a prayer of appreciation and gratitude that acknowledges this good, life-affirming element of my life.

Experiencing love on this deeper level, that is, that special place within the soul that yearns for connection with the divine, opens me up to receive the spirit of life as it pours into me, and reciprocally, I feel liberated to give more of myself in lovingkindness to my wife and the world.

The capacity for a disciplined prayer life develops over time. As with any other endeavor, we become better as we put in more time. If you practice daily, you are more likely to become spiritually attuned to prayer than if you practice monthly, or without any sense of regularity. My sense is that prayer is the most rewarding spiritual discipline for those seeking depth in their inner lives. For those who commit to prayer, it can be truly transformative.

My Journey of Prayer

Early in my ministry, I thought of myself as a prayer maven. I developed my style of prayer by listening to the prayers of a favorite minister on television. (Not a televangelist of the get rich quick ilk!) I loved to pray, and it showed. Friends and colleagues frequently called upon me to pray at church, meals, and other gatherings. Prayer brought out my creativity and connection with the holy. Praying in public helped me to help others develop their own prayer lives and expand their understanding of prayer as a spiritual discipline available to all, not just clergy. The only advantage that I'd had was confidence that my prayer style was simple enough to touch the hearts of many people and down-to-earth enough to convey the concerns of everyday living. In reality, that advantage was available to all who were willing to take the life of prayer seriously. Most importantly, prayer helped me deepen my faith as I realized more and more that I needed to live a life that reflected the prayers I recited.

As my spiritual life has evolved, transitioning from the United Methodist Church tradition to the Unitarian Universalist faith, so did my approach to prayer. My prayer now tends to be more internalized and integrated with my life. That simply means that I make my daily activities so coherent with my prayer life that I'm perpetually creating active, enlivening love in real-time. I've also revised how I understand prayer and how I distinguish the holy. Earlier in my spiritual life, I envisioned God as a being I'd be constantly appealing to, asking for intercession on behalf of others.

Now, I view God as the seat of my consciousness, no longer a being that lives beyond me. More importantly, God is not a being within me, but a sense of radiating awareness that guides me.

I do not pray to myself—that might border on idolatry. Often, I do not pray at all. But I am aware of many spiritual manifestations of prayer in and around me. In this manner, my prayer life has evolved alongside my understanding of the divine.

Chapter 23

Reconciliation

Much of the prayer spoken into the universe arises from our sense of brokenness. We are people of broken relationships, cutoffs, and irreconcilable differences. Prayer is a primary means of expressing our desire for reconciliation. There is hardly a better feeling than being reunited with someone who you deeply care about and were once at odds with than to never have been separated in the first place. The havoc that conflict and disagreement wreak on our lives is often never repaired, but it can be with the will to reconcile on the part of both parties. Having gone through heart-wrenching separations with dear friends, even with my mother at one point, I know this firsthand. Reconciliation is difficult, but it is usually well worth the effort. The persistence that is required for reconciliation is, perhaps, what makes it a spiritual discipline.

Reconciliation is the repair of brokenness that we feel when we are separated from others or misunderstood. People who get a hold of their faith understand that human beings have an innate desire to receive care and to be needed. When such feelings are violated, we experience dissonance and conflict. Unfortunately, life does not usually prepare us with the skills to negotiate difficult conditions. We rely on instinct. Others will depend on tactics learned early in life that are no longer effective. The offices of psychologists and other mental health counselors are filled with people who have developed issues (for example, depression), or live at low levels of functioning (for example, conflict avoidance) due to their inability to navigate difficult situations with others. For the wellbeing of our spiritual selves, it is essential to engage in this discipline, as necessary, if one is to grow into exemplary faith.

Steps Toward Reconciliation

I believe that reconciliation begins in the heart, whereby one who is ripe with a genuine desire and is grounded in concern for the other, dares to reconcile with their counterpart. Without heartfelt concern, which I translate as the willingness to extend compassion, acknowledgment, and forgiveness—both for our part and theirs—there is little possibility of trusting that the relationship could be restored. With such an earnest concern in place, I believe that you are in a better position to create a climate where healing and growth is possible. The open heart lends itself to safety so that people can speak freely and openly about difficult issues.

Next, it is good to develop an interest in the other person and their needs. Often, the lack of interest in another causes the fissure in the first place. It is my practice to listen to the other person deeply. But we have to be interested enough to listen well with care. At my church, we acknowledge that when someone is unhappy about something in the church there is usually an underlying issue at stake. Anger, conflict, or confusion is only a cover for the real issue. Listening to the other with a deep interest in their story, without interruption, often opens a space for the real issue to surface. Developing curiosity about the other's needs also helps you tease out their true concerns.

It helps to give yourself permission to step back and hold the issue at arm's length and resist the urge to defend yourself amid reconciliation. Often, we are too close to the problem in the first place, or we *are* the problem! You can easily determine this by asking yourself if you are capable of listening to the other and allowing them to speak without interrupting them. If you are so entangled or enmeshed that this is not possible, then in all likelihood you'll need more emotional distancing before being able to proceed with reconciliation. In pastoral psychology terms, we call this state *undifferentiated*. Your task is to become more differentiated, to be able to be a calm, solid, yet connected person during a dynamic situation. This takes a lot of personal work (that is beyond the scope of this book), but it is well worth it. For now, suffice it to say that if in your process of reconciliation you find yourself fighting tooth and nail with the other person, you are at the opposite end of the differentiation spectrum of being a solid, connected self. By remembering to keep calm and connected and put the other's needs ahead of your own, you can begin to turn yourself around.

Finally, as Thurman encourages in *Disciplines*, build an awareness "For a kind of personal activity in relatedness that may inspire another person to open the door, to turn toward one." Put another way, what can you do to encourage the other person to seek you out, or at least be receptive to your invitation to reconcile. Often, this is simply a matter of saying to the estranged person or group that you are available and willing to restore yourself to the right relationship. If the other is in a similar place, then you're well on your way. If not, you may need to make more concrete and overt efforts to garner their attention and rebuild trust. Wherever you are on that continuum, I encourage you to push through and don't let anything keep you from full reconciliation.

An Example of Reconciliation

Here is an example of reconciliation that I've helped to negotiate. While the actual reconciliation was within a group, I believe actual personal transformation occurred as well. My congregation has a network of covenant groups that are organized and guided by a four-person steering team. A covenant group is a small, supportive community of people meeting regularly for spiritual and emotional sharing and discussion. When one covenant group fell out of good standing with the steering team, several new members were driven away. Those members, feeling put off by the group, had reported their ill feelings to the steering team, who in turn made several unsuccessful attempts to resolve the situation.

The covenant group appeared unwilling to make any change in conducting meetings or its relationship with the steering team. They would not meet with the steering team member assigned to them as a partner, nor give any indication of modifying their procedures and practices. Finally, the steering team concluded there were no options available to them, other than to discontinue the covenant group's formal connection to the network. The covenant group could continue to meet, but not under the auspices of the church. The steering team sent the covenant group a message to that effect, which suddenly piqued the covenant group's interest—but only enough for them to hunker down into their position. Then, the covenant group realized that they *did* want to remain connected to the covenant group network instead of being banished to the sidelines of the program.

As a staff partner to the steering team, I invited them to make use of a team at the church called the Healthy Congregations Committee (HCC), whose purpose is to help reconcile and repair such conflicts. They agreed. I also called the covenant group leader and invited her to join the process. Likewise, she agreed on behalf of the covenant group. There was one snag: one person belonged to both the steering team and the covenant group. He recused himself from the process, though he maintained a highly differentiated posture throughout the reconciliation. Kudos to him!

The HCC is exceptionally capable and skillful in these moments, each one of them is calm, solid, and connected with self in his or her own right. They encouraged the steering team to be thoughtful and open-hearted in their communications with the covenant group. This included a series of emails, then a more formal negotiation of efforts through a series of formal letters between the steering team and the covenant group. The HCC helped the steering team create the tone suggesting an open heart and genuine desire to reconcile on their part. As a result, the environment was ripe for constructive dialogue and healing. Both parties worked through their important concerns, listening to the others' positions, developing interest in the other, gaining a better understanding, and creating mutual respect for each other's needs. To be honest, it was a lengthy process, taking a few months, several meetings, working through disagreements, and finding common ground and language while standing in a shared faith tradition. It was sometimes arduous, but always promising, and it ended in a reconciled state for both parties. The covenant group, fortunately, remained in the network.

I confessed to having had a personal sense of reconciliation with the group myself. As a minister, I aimed for healthy boundaries with my parishioners. While not avoiding conflict, I also strived for collaboration instead of telling people what to do. Some situations demand a firm, more directive approach—otherwise, things may not get done. In the situation I've described, I did speak as a representative for the steering team on one occasion. Fortunately, I've only spoken what I knew to be factual. But speaking as their representative casted me as a slightly oppositional force to what the covenant group was trying to do as a self-directed group. In reality, I was trying to bring awareness of the church's policies rather than take a side. Wanting to be in a civil relationship with both parties meant that I had to avoid taking sides and stay in a neutral position throughout the process. But I couldn't help at times feeling that I might be perceived as "the man" bringing down the hammer. I worked diligently to remain neutral, positive, and prayerful in all of my interactions with both parties. In the end, I, too, felt reconciled and in a good standing relationship with everyone involved.

At its heart, therefore, reconciliation is all about relationality and building a deeper human connection. We all need encounter strong relationships along our path to getting a hold of our faith. Inevitably, though, things will sometimes go awry despite our best intentions. The path to reconciliation is usually open. I hesitate to say *always* because I know that cutoffs (chronically broken relationships) do occur and often all attempts at reconciliation fail. Yet, if we are willing to maintain a spirit of reconciliation about ourselves, we find that there is hope in this broken world of wholeness.

Chapter 24

Spiritual Journaling

I have learned that I've grown spiritually by reflecting upon my experiences of being with people, the divine presence, and nature. Often, I've reflected on what ordinarily might seem mundane, and through these reflections, the mundane has taken on a spiritual manifestation. The insight I've drawn was transformative, illustrating not only unity among all things in creation, but also fundamental longings and desires in common to all people.

When I read Thurman's spiritual journaling, I observe him working out complex problems. For instance such as love and conflict among persons, war and peace, nonviolent protests in the face of racism and oppression, and, of course, individual pursuits to know God. In some books, Thurman was meticulous about categorizing his reflections. No matter the category, a thread of relationality and religious experience had ran through the center of his work. Journaling was Thurman's primary means of sharing his overwhelming encounters with God in a manner that his readers could appreciate and imitate.

Spiritual Journaling and Spiritual Practices

In his book *Deep is the Hunger*, Thurman asks a series of questions to highlight the purposes and end goals of spiritual practices.

1. "What is the significance of spiritual exercises?"

2. "Precisely what is prayer and how does one pray?"

3. "What techniques and methods are available for deepening one's sense of the presence of God and how may one work in the world courageously and intelligently on behalf of a decent world, without despair and complete fatigue?"

4. "What are the resources for personal rehabilitation and renewal?"

Brilliantly, the questions also imply their answers. For example, the third question suggests to the reader that spiritual disciplines will deepen the sense that God is present in one's life. It also asserts that we should seek ways to be courageous and intelligent as we go about doing our work in the world. The final question implies that we need to find resources, or spiritual practices, which offer rehabilitation and renewal. I've discovered that people of strong faith, by and large, *know and practice* the answers to these questions. At some stage in their lives, the answers become a part of their identity.

Spiritual journaling is a perfect means to reflect on the questions above or your inquiry. Many people, including me, find it easier to pursue such intimate questions on paper rather than in conversation. Journaling gives you time to experiment with your thoughts and feelings and fine-tune your positions and sentiments. Plus, when writing the answers, you are free to go deeper with your responses and add contour to your thoughts about your practice.

In reality, spiritual journaling need not be about answering questions as much as a means to offload feelings, thoughts, and experiences that shape who you are as a person. I recall using spiritual journaling daily while going through a divorce. There were so many thoughts traversing my mind and spirit during that period that I needed to get them out and down on paper. I found the practice to be cathartic on many levels. I wrote about my disappointment with myself and my ex-spouse, my fears, but also about the future that was unfolding right in front of me. At night, when I was alone and it was quiet, I'd sit down and scribble on paper whatever came to mind; sometimes, only for a few minutes. But it was always enough for me to connect with my deeper feelings, experiences, and with God. I am convinced that spiritual journaling had kept me from falling into a pit of despair, anger, or depression. It was a saving grace.

The main requirements to learn from spiritual journaling are about motivation and trusting that the discipline of the work will pay dividends. These days, it is easier to journal than ever. You only have to open a new page on your computer and begin writing. (I didn't own a PC for most of my journaling!) You can do it on a napkin! Some people say writing with a pen helps people connect better with their thoughts and emotions. To be a gifted writer, there aren't any requirements. After all, you are writing to an audience of one—you. There is no need to write perfectly. Whatever you put down is fine. Who knows? One day you may want to publish your memoirs. If so, you'll have some good material. Until then, just put your pen, smartphone, tablet, or PC where your faith is and believe in the process. Get busy writing!

Chapter 25

Community

I view all persons as members of the earth's greater community and fellowship. As people who cherish sacred and secular texts from a variety of faith traditions, and engage in interfaith dialogue as an ongoing practice, I believe that we all can exemplify the community-building ideals that we seek out, especially those in the social justice arena. Being with others, especially in the service of the ultimate and in the search for peace, each of us can bring together people from diverse backgrounds. So, they might collectively experience unity of the spirit and take that experience out into the world.

From Thurman's approach, we learn an integral lesson for our spiritual journey: mature and seasoned faith takes us beyond our self-interest and into the broader sphere of human enterprises. We forgo the community-building aspect of our faith at our peril.

After a mystical experience in India, Thurman committed himself to put his dream of community-building into action. He describes that vision as follows:

"We knew that we must test whether a religious fellowship could be developed in America that was capable of cutting across all racial barriers, with a carry-over into the common life, a fellowship that would later alter the behavioral patterns of those involved."

This vision highlighted his desire to merge theology with practice. It also demonstrated his desire to broadcast his vision of relationship and actualize it in a diverse body of worship. He keenly understood that faith which did not mature into real interaction and concrete behaviors between people in everyday life, was, at best, a weak faith. I, too, am convinced that the true mark of faith is a visible relationality that is experienced and nurtured to its mature state.

Thurman grounded his vision on a solid religious tradition dating back to the New England Puritans. They established a pattern for forming church communities and insisted that the true mark of relationality amongst church members was the transformation of belief into action. In a discussion concerning the constitution of a church, the Unitarian Universalist historian Conrad Wright argued the exact point Thurman put forth, saying:

"So it was that when the New England Puritans gathered their churches, they wrote covenants, by which the members agreed to walk together in mutual fellowship, in commitment to one another as well as to Christ Jesus, who was recognized as the supreme Lord of his Church. They acknowledged that under some circumstances the covenant might be implicit; to be discerned not in a document but in a way people behave in *relation* to one another."

The emphasis is on a relationship as a transformative power in moving persons toward a deeper faith through the development of community.

Making Community Real

To make this real, in 1944 Thurman and Alfred Fisk, a Presbyterian pastor, founded the Church for the Fellowship of All Peoples in San Francisco, California. The church was deliberately unaffiliated with any single denominational body so it would have the greatest opportunity for diversity—racially, denominationally, and ethnically. The community flourished, with Thurman and Fisk alternately assuming preaching responsibilities. At its peak, membership reached about three hundred fifty persons, and another thousand supported the fellowship financially. Though still a viable congregation with an ongoing ministry, its numbers have declined over the years, and I imagine that it has followed the trend of many congregations.

Pastoral theologian Zoë Bennett Moore's useful framework for understanding community brings together the joint intentions of Thurman and Fisk. She identifies three components of community that honor the diversity and practice that the Fellowship of All Peoples embodied.

> The first...is an image of a central commitment which holds things and people together by attraction to the center rather than by a policing of the boundaries. Second, inclusiveness is of itself a gospel value, and as such is more important than doctrinal, political, or moral correctness. Indeed, commitments to *love* and to *grace* as primary are themselves doctrinal, political, and commitments. Third, vigorous witness to our perspective on the truth does not entail the silencing or exclusion of those with whom we disagree, of those from different social or religious backgrounds, or of those whose own witness is different.

By turning their vision of a collected community into a real group of people who dwelled together in fellowship in an established house of worship, Thurman and Fisk demonstrated their commitment to community. By their collaboration, as they shared the pulpit and worked to establish an ongoing legacy of their vision through church growth and continuity beyond the church's physical walls, they bequeathed their commitment to future generations. Having the fellowship intentionally remain autonomous rather than aligning with a particular denominational body, Thurman and Fisk established an ecclesiastical reality that made inclusivity one of its highest aims. In these ways, Thurman's theology of love became a practical reality that was lived out in a community determined to bear witness to the grace and love amongst its members. Finally, as co-pastors of the Church for the Fellowship of All Peoples, Fisk and Thurman modeled a democratic leadership style for all to see— within and beyond the congregation. The pastors' mixed denominational heritage demonstrated their commitment to social and religious equality and authored a spirit of ecumenism that encouraged and valued all voices.

Making This Practical for You

You don't have to start at a new church to practice community. Anywhere you are in the company of others, especially those you meet with regularly, can be mindful that you are a community. Whether you have two, three, or twenty people, you are in community. Scriptures remind us that the spirit of life is always present. So even with just two human beings present, the spirit makes three! Your task then is to create a spirit of unity amongst yourselves and acknowledge that what you do together is in the service of God, the universe, or the greater good.

The practice of community-building mainly requires that you be mindful of this objective and build into your work and time together a mission statement, covenant, or agreement that makes your intentions real. For example, if you are interested in starting a mentoring group for young people in your neighborhood or church, it would be helpful to start with the idea that your work with youth is a form of community-building. You may draft up some guiding principles or a mission statement for your group specifying that the group is in support of the community it belongs to, and aims to be a community that supports its members.

Here is a fictional example of such a covenant: The Downtown Mentors consist of men and boys that meet bi-weekly to create a safe community in fellowship together and discuss the spiritual principles of leadership, service, and responsibility. With this simple statement of purpose, the group adopts an intentional stance for building a community that serves not only the men and boys in the group, but the community where they live and the broader community for the work that they do together. This occurs organically as the group members learn and grow together, take their communal spirit into the world, and spread their "good news" to all they meet. To make it more formal, each member might be given a copy of the mission statement, and be asked to keep it in mind, memorize it, and agree to abide by it when the group meets. Making it a way of life. This may sound a bit drastic, but this is how an intention becomes a spiritual practice and integrates into your faith.

This is but one example of how you can build community. Likely, you are already in communities doing this type of spiritual practice, such as the scouts, Habitat for Humanity, the YMCA, various church groups, neighborhood watch, hiking groups, etc. The trick is to bring the community-building aspect to the consciousness of the group's members. Lifting up the community aspect is a clear way of showing that our spiritual work goes beyond the self, the family, and our tribe or clan. It is a way of demonstrating that spiritual practice is ultimately for the world, to make the world the one that we dream of.

Chapter 26

Summary

Each of us, as we journey along our spiritual path, has the same capacity to include any of these spiritual practices into our lives. Much of the work lies in maintaining an awareness that these practices are already a part of our lives, and are helping us to experience transcendence regularly. I believe that within each of us lies the capacity to be an example of strong faith. Can you imagine yourself as a faith leader yet? Hopefully, by now you are already putting your faith into action. When it comes down to it, every little step in the right direction makes a big difference. Eventually, if you stay on the path, you will get to where you're going.

Back to Relationality (relationships)

It is through our direct encounter with the divine, the universe, nature, and each other that we can construct relationality, that is, relationships that enable our faith experience to coalesce. Seeing the unity of persons, groups, and societies through the lens of mysticism is a framework that helps us understand the interrelatedness of our inner lives with the external world. As grand as it sounds, each of us has a role in this, as we live it out in our relationships with each other and the world.

We've explored mysticism and spiritual practices and witnessed their breadth and depth. I've encouraged a host of faith practices: commitment to your faith life, mindfulness, growth, acknowledgment of suffering, prayer, reconciliation, and spiritual journaling. These are faith practices that can become important resources to summon up during times of trial. Through them, we discover within ourselves and our relationship with God, a way of experiencing transcendence and triumph, even when our "backs are against the wall." These resources are not limited to our individual practice, but can also be used in community, as we share our stories and find strength and hope together. The more you practice, the more you grow. And as you grow, your faith grows too.

Thank you for reading my book. If you enjoyed it, won't you please take a moment to leave me a review at your favorite retailer?

Also, please get a copy of my first book, *It's Your World*, which is a combination of memoir and social commentary that will open your mind to new ways of seeing and experiencing your world. If you have children or just enjoy children's books, I've written two books for you. The titles are *Hank and the Runaway Catfish* and *Finding Your Way Home.* All of these titles will be available in eBook and paperback.

Thanks!

Xolani Kacela

About the Author

Xolani "xk" Kacela, Ph.D. serves as the Minister, Unitarian Universalist Church of Las Cruces, New Mexico. The congregation welcomes all people with the motto: "May we convey love in all we do." He also serves as a chaplain in the New Mexico Air National Guard, based in Albuquerque, NM. Prior to that, he served with the District of Columbia National Guard at Joint Base Andrews and worked at U.S. Special Operations Command at MacDill Air Force Base in Tampa, FL. He began his military career with the Texas Air National Guard in Ft. Worth, TX. He has deployed four times, including service during Operation Iraqi Freedom.

Xolani enjoys many hobbies with his favorite being hanging out with his wife and partner, Tamara. Together, they could make their own outdoors reality show. They're constantly looking for their next adventure. They've enjoyed ice fishing, bowfishing, and hunting deer, Javelina, and Oryx.

Check out the website and blog, revdrxk.com (https://revdrxk.com/). Also, be sure to read the interview with the author (https://www.smashwords.com/interview/xkacela).

You can find xk's other writings on his sister website, MasteringYourOwnFaith.com, and you can reach him at xk@revdrxk.com.

Connect with me:

Follow me on Twitter

(https://twitter.com/XolaniKacela)

Friend me on Facebook

(https://www.facebook.com/revdrxk/posts
116109173469533)

Follow me on YouTube

(https://www.youtube.com/channel/UCjOjpXa-
VW4oNuvJw_9ytkQ?view_as=subscriber)

BIBLIOGRAPHY

Alley, Linetta S. "Listening for God's Call in One's Life." *Brethren Life and Thought* 46, no. 3-4 (Summer-Fall 2001): 145-149.

Altany, Alan. "What Makes a Mystic?" *U.S. Catholic* 57, no. 11 (Nov 1992): 30.

Anderson, E. Byron. "A Constructive Task in Religious Education: Making Christian Selves." *Religious Education* 93, no. 2 (Spring 1998): 173-189.

Anderson, Harlene. "On a Roller Coaster: A Collaborative Language Systems Approach to Therapy." In *The New Language of Change: Constructive Collaboration in Psychotherapy*, ed. Steven Friedman, 323-344. New York: Guilford, 1993.

Ashby, Homer U., Jr. *Our Home is Over Jordan: A Black Pastoral Theology.* St. Louis: Chalice, 2003.

Bauermeister, Paul. "Mate Selection: Cupid's Three Level Radar and Why It Does Not Always Work." *Currents in Theology and Mission* 11, no. 4 (August 1984): 227-232.

Bennett, Charles. *A Philosophical Study of Mysticism.* New Haven: Yale University, 1931.

Berger, Jennifer G. "Living Postmodernism: The Complex Balance of Worldview and Developmental Capacity." *Revision* 27, no. 4 (Spring 2005): 20-27.

Black, Helen K. "Poverty and Prayer: Spiritual Narratives of Elderly African-American Women." *Review of Religious Research* 40 (June 1999): 359-375.

Boyd, Glenn E. "Pastoral Counseling: Relational Listening and Open-Ended Questions." *Pastoral Psychology* 51, no. 5 (May 2003): 345-360.

Braxton, Brad R. *No Longer Slaves: Galatians and African American Experience.* Collegeville: Liturgical, 2002.

Brueggemann, Walter. *The Prophetic Imagination.* Philadelphia: Fortress, 1978.

Burwash, Rev. N., S.T.D. *Wesley's 52 Standard Sermons.* Salem, OH: Schmul, 1988.

Butler, Lee H. "African-American Pastoral Psychology in the Twenty-First Century Will Be More Than Sensual Healing." *Journal of Religious Thought* 54, no. 1 (1997): 113-130.

________. "The Unpopular Experience of Popular Culture: Cultural Resistance as Identity Formation." *Journal of Pastoral Theology* 11, no. 1 (June 2001): 40-52.

Callum, Neville. "Hope: A Caribbean Perspective." *Ecumenical Review* 50, no. 2 (April 1998): 137-142.

Carlsen, Mary Baird. *Meaning-Making: Therapeutic Processes in Adult Development.* New York: W. W. Norton, 1988.

Cartwright, John H. "The Religious Ethics of Howard Thurman." *Annual of the Society of Christian Ethics* 5, no. 1 (1985): 79-99.

Cone, Cecil. *The Identity Crisis in Black Theology.* Nashville: African Methodist Episcopal Church, 1975.

Devor, N. G. "Toward a Relational Voice of Faith." Ph. D. diss., Boston University, 1989.

Deyoung, Curtiss Paul, M.O. Emerson, K.C Kim, G. Yancey. *United by Faith: The Multiracial Congregation as an Answer to the Problem of Race*. New York Oxford, 2003.

Dicken, E. W. Trueman. "Teresa of Jesus and John of the Cross." In *The Study of Spirituality*, ed. Cheslyn Jones, G. Wainwright, & E. Yarnold, SJ, 363-376. New York: Oxford, 1986.

Dunn, Dana. *The Practical Researcher: A Student Guide to Conducting Psychological Research*. Boston: McGraw-Hill, 1999.

Dykstra, Craig. "Looking Ahead at Theological Education." *Theological Education* 28, no. 1 (Autumn 1991): 95-105.

Dykstra, Craig. *Growing in the Life of Faith: Education and Christian Practices*. Louisville: Geneva, 1999.

Eriksen, Karen. "The Constructive Developmental Theory of Robert Kegan." *The Family Journal* 14, no. 3 (July 2006): 290-298.

______. "Robert Kegan, Ph.D: Subject-Object Theory and Family Therapy." *The Family Journal* 14, no. 3 (July 2006): 299-305.

______. "Counseling the 'Imperial' Client: Translating Robert Kegan." *The Family Journal* 15, no. 2 (April 2007): 174-182.

Eyre, Ronald. "An Interview with Howard Thurman and Ronald Eyre." *Theology Today* 38, no. 2 (July 1981): 208-213.

Fish, Stanley. *Doing What Comes Naturally: Change, Rhetoric, and the Practice of Theory in Literary and Legal Studies.* Durham: Duke, 1989.

Floyd-Thomas, Stacey M. and Laura Gillman. "The Whole Story is What I'm After": Womanist Revolutions and Liberation Feminist Revelations Through Biomythography and Emancipatory Historiography." *Black Theology* 3, no. 2 (July 2005): 176-199.

Fluker, Walter Earl. "They Looked for a City: A Comparison of the Idea of Community in Howard Thurman and Martin Luther King, Jr.," *Journal of Religious Ethics* 18, no. 2 (Fall 1990): 33-55.

Fowler, James W. *Stages of Faith.* San Francisco: Harper & Row, 1981.

Genero, Nancy P., J. B. Miller, J. Surrey, and L. M. Baldwin. "Measuring Perceived Mutuality in Close Relationship: Validation of the Mutual Psychological Development Questionnaire." *Journal of Family Psychology* 6, no. 1 (1992): 36-48.

Gill-Austern, Brita L. "Pedagogy Under the Influence of Feminism and Womanism." In *Feminist & Womanist Pastoral Theology,* eds. Bonnie J. Miller-McLemore and Brita L. Gill-Austern, 149-168. Nashville: Abingdon, 1999.

Goldberg, Michael. *Theology and Narrative: A Critical Introduction.* Nashville: Abingdon, 1991.

Goodwin, Mary E. "Racial Roots and Religion: An Interview with Howard Thurman." *Christian Century* 90, no. 19 (May 9, 1973): 532-535.

Gordon, Walter I. "The Nat Turner Insurrection Trials." *Black Renaissance/Renaissance Noire* 6, no. 3 (Spring-Summer 2006): 132-138.

Gore, Jonathan S., S. E. Cross, and M.L. Morris. "Let's Be Friends: Relational Self-Construal and Development of Intimacy." *Personal Relationships* 13 (2006): 83-102.

Gorsuch, Nancy J. *Introducing Feminist Pastoral Care and Counseling.* Cleveland: Pilgrim, 2001.

Graham, Elaine L. *Transforming Practice.* Eugene, OR: Wipf and Stock, 1996.

Graham, Larry Kent. *Care of Persons, Care of Worlds.* Nashville: Abingdon, 1992.

Gray, Thomas. "The Confessions of Nat Turner, the Leader of the Late Insurrection in Southampton, Virginia [book on-line] (Washington, D.C.: Library of Congress Rare Book and Special Collections Division, African American Odyssey, 1832, accessed 1 August 2007); available from http://docsouth.unc/neh/turner/turner.html; Internet.

Grenz, Stanley L. "Eschatological Theology: Contours of a Postmodern Theology of Hope." *Review and Expository* 97 (2000): 339-354.

Grenz, Stanley L. and Roger E. Olson. *20th Century Theology: God & the World in a Transitional Age.* Downers Grove: InterVarsity, 1992.

Guthrie, Shirley C., Jr. *Christian Doctrine*. Atlanta: John Knox, 1968.

Harding, Vincent "God's Avenging Scourge." *Christian History* 18, no. 2 (1999): 28-35.

Henig, Robin Marantz. "Darwin's God." *The New York Times Magazine*, March 4, 2007, 36-85.

Hogue, David A. *Remembering the Future, Imagining the Past: Story, Ritual, and the Human Brain*. Cleveland: Pilgrim, 2003.

Holifield, E. Brooks. "How History Informs Selfhood Learning to Value the Past." *Christian Century* 93, no. 4 (February 4-11, 1976): 93-95.

Hubert, Susan. "Testimony and Prophecy in *The Life and Religious Experience of Jarena Lee.*" *Journal of Religious Thought* 55, no. 1 (Spring/Fall 1998): 45-53.

Hunsinger, Deborah van Deusen. "Paying Attention: The Art of Listening." *Christian Century* 123, no. 17 (August 22, 2006): 24 30.

Ignelzi, Michael. "Meaning-Making in the Learning and Teaching Process." *New Directions for Teaching and Learning* 82, (Summer 2000): 5-14.

Immink, F. Gerrit. *Faith: A Practical Theological Reconstruction.* Grand Rapids: William B. Eerdmans, 2005.

Iser, Wolfgang. "The Reading Process: A Phenomenological Approach.," In *Reader-Response Criticism: From Formalism to Post-Structuralism*, ed. Jane P. Tompkins, 50-69. Baltimore: Johns Hopkins University, 1980.

Jones, Timothy Paul. "The Necessity of Objective Assent in the Act of Christian Faith." *Bibliotheca Sacra* 162 (April-June 2005): 150-157.

Jordan, Judith V. *Relational Development: Therapeutic Implications of Empathy and Shame.* Wellesley, MA: Stone Center, 1989.

__________ "A Relational-Cultural Model: Healing through mutual empathy." *Bulletin of the Menninger Clinic* 65, no. 1 (Winter 2001): 92-103.

Kegan, Robert. "Meaning Making: The Constructive-Development Approach to Persons and Practice." *Personnel & Guidance Journal* 58, no. 5 (Jan 80): 373-381.

__________. *The Evolving Self.* Cambridge: Harvard, 1982.

__________. *In Over Our Heads.* Cambridge, MA: Harvard, 1994.

__________. "Epistemology, Expectation, and Aging." In *Handbook of Aging and Mental Health: An Integrative Approach*, ed. Jacob Lomranz, 197-216. New York: Plenum, 1998.

Kelcourse, Felicity B., ed. *Human Development and Faith: Life-Cycle Stages of Body, Mind, and Soul.* St. Louis: Chalice 2004.

Kinghorn, Kevin. *The Decision of Faith: Can Christian Beliefs be Freely Chosen?* New York: T&T Clark, 2005.

Kopas, Jane. "Something Particular: Women's Self Narratives as a Resource for Theology." In *Themes in Feminist Theology for the New Millennium (I)*, ed. Francis A. Eigo, 1-34. Villanova: Villanova Univ., 2002.

Lamy, John. "Find Your Stage of Consciousness." *Spirituality and Health* (January-February 2008): 35-67.

Lartey, Emmanuel Y. *Pastoral Theology in an Intercultural World.* Cleveland: Pilgrim, 2006.

Lee, Jarena. "Religious Experience and Journal of Mrs. Jarena Lee." In *Spiritual Narratives*, ed. Susan Houchins. New York: Oxford, 1988.

Leith, John H. *Basic Christian Doctrine.* Louisville: Westminster John Knox, 1993.

Lester, Andrew D. *Hope in Pastoral Counseling.* Louisville: Westminster John Knox, 1995.

______. *The Angry Christian: A Theology for Care and Counseling.* Louisville: Westminster John Knox, 2003.

Lester, Andrew D. and Howard Stone. "Hope and Possibility: Envisioning the Future in Pastoral Conversation." *Journal of Pastoral Care* 55, no. 3 (Fall 2001): 259-269.

Liebert, Elizabeth. *Changing Life Patterns: Adult Development in Spiritual Direction.* St. Louis: Chalice, 2000.

"Love in the Time of Dementia," *New York Times*, 18 November 2007, Week in Review, p. 1, 3.

Love, Patrick G. and Victoria L. Guthrie. "Kegan's Orders of Consciousness." *New Directions for Student Services* 88 (Winter 99): 65-77.

Maddox, Randy L. *Responsible Grace: John Wesley's Practical Theology.* Nashville: Kingswood, 1994.

Marshall, Ellen Ott, ed. *Choosing Peace Through Daily Practices*. Cleveland: Pilgrim, 2005.

Marshall, Joretta L. "Covenants and Partnerships: Pastoral Counseling with Women in Lesbian Relationships" (Work in Progress). *Journal of Pastoral Theology* 5, no. (Summer 1995): 81-93.

Marty, Martin E. Marty. "Mysticism and the Religious Quest for Freedom" *Christian Century* 100, no. 8 (March 16, 1983): 242-246.

Matthaei, Sondra Higgins. "Rethinking Faith Formation." *Religious Education* 99, no. 1 (Winter 2004): 56-70.

McKanan, Dan. *Identifying the Image of God: Radical Christians and Nonviolent Power in the Antebellum United States*. New York: Oxford, 2002.

Miller-McLemore, Bonnie. "Feminist Theory in Pastoral Theology." In *Feminist & Womanist Pastoral Theology*, eds. Bonnie J. Miller-McLemore & Brita L. Gill-Austern, 77-94. Nashville: Abingdon, 1999.

Moore, Zoë Bennett. *Introducing Feminist Perspectives on Pastoral Theology*. Cleveland: Pilgrim, 2002.

Moschella, Mary Clark. *Living Devotions: Reflections on Immigration, Identity, and Religious Imagination*. Eugene: Pickwick, 2008.

Neuger, Christie Cozad "Women and Relationality." In *Feminist & Womanist Pastoral Theology*, eds. Bonnie J. Miller-McLemore & Brita L. Gill-Austern, 113-132. Nashville: Abingdon, 1999.

________. *Counseling Women: A Narrative, Pastoral Approach.* Minneapolis: Fortress, 2001.

Norris, Kathleen. "Standing on Promises." *Christian Century* 122, no. 24 (November 29, 2005): 21.

Olson, R. Paul. *The Reconciled Life: A Critical Theory of Counseling.* Peabody, MA: Hendrickson, 1997.

Oman, Doug and Carl E. Thoresen. "Spiritual Modeling: A Key to Spiritual and Religious Growth?" *The International Journal for the Psychology of Religion* 13, no. 3 (2003): 149-165.

Ortberg, John. "Hunger for Joy." *Christian Century* 124, no. 18 (September 4, 2007): 39.

Otto, Rudolf. *Mysticism East and West.* New York: Macmillan, 1932.

Outler, Albert C. *John Wesley.* New York: Oxford, 1964.

Overstreet, H.A. *The Mature Mind.* New York: W. W. Norton, 1949.

Owen-Towle, Tom. *FreeThinking Mystics with Hands.* Boston: Skinner House Books, 1998.

Paris, Peter. *The Spirituality of African Peoples.* Minneapolis, Fortress, 1995.

Parks, Sharon Daloz. *Big Questions, Worthy Dreams: Mentoring Young Adults in Their Search for Meaning, Purpose, and Faith.* San Francisco: Jossey-Bass, 2000.

Patton, John. *Pastoral Care in Context: An Introduction to Pastoral Care.* Louisville: Westminster John Knox Press, 1993.

Pierce, Yolanda. *Hell Without Fires: Slavery, Christianity, and the Antebellum Spiritual Narrative.* Gainesville: University Press of Florida, 2005.

Pinnock, Clark H. "Divine Relationality: A Pentecostal Contribution to the Doctrine of God." *Journal of Pentecostal Theology* 16 (April 2000): 3-26.

Placher, William. "Teaching Moments." *Christian Century* 122, no. 4 (February 22, 2005): 22-23.

Pollard, Alton, III. *Mysticism and Social Change: The Social Witness of Howard Thurman.* New York: P. Lang, 1992.

Pudaloff, Ross J. "No Change Without Purchase: Olaudah Equiano and the Economics of Self and Market." *Early American Literature* 40, no. 3 (September 2005): 499-527.

Raboteau, Albert J. "Slave Autonomy and Religion." *Journal of Religious Thought* 38, no. 2 (Fall 1981/Winter 1982): 51-64.

______. "The Secret Religion of Slaves." *Christian History* 11, no. 1 (1992): 42-46.

Raboteau, Albert J., C. Sanders, R. L. Stevenson, Jr. "The Dignity of Faith." *Christian History* 18, no. 2 (1999): 42-46.

Ramsay, Nancy J. *Pastoral Diagnosis: A Resource for Ministries of Care and Counseling.* Minneapolis: Fortress, 1998.

Roberts, J. Deotis Sr. Review of *Who Trusts in God: Musings on the Meaning of Providence*, by Albert C. Outler. *Journal of the American Academy of Religion* 38, no. 1 (March 1970): 114-115.

Roehlkepartain, Eugene C. "What Makes Faith Mature?" *Christian Century* 107, no. 16 (May 9, 199): 496-499.

Rosenborough, David J. "Coming Out Stories Framed as Faith Narrative, or Stories of Spiritual Growth." *Pastoral Psychology* 55 (2006): 47-59.

Schipani, Daniel S. *The Way of Wisdom in Pastoral Counseling.* Elkhart, IN: Institute of Mennonite Studies, 2003.

Schneider, Mary France. "A Narrative Dialogue: An Interview with Jill Freedman and Gene Combs." *Journal of Individual Psychology* 54, no. 4 (Winter 1998): 416-430.

Slee, Nicola. *Women's Faith Development: Patterns and Process.* Ashgate: Burlington, VT, 2004.

Slocum, Robert. B. "Kingdom Come: Preliminaries for a Relational Theology of Hope." *Anglican Theological Review* 82. no. 3 (Summer 2000): 571-578.

Smith, Archie Jr., "Hospitality: A Spiritual Resource for Building Community." *Journal of the Interdenominational Theological Center* 25, no. 3 (Spring 1998): 139-151.

Springsted, Eric O. *The Act of Faith: Christian Faith and the Moral Self.* Grand Rapids: Eerdmans, 2002.

Stewart, Carlyle Fielding III. *God, Being, and Liberation: A Comparative Analysis of the Theologies and Ethics of James H. Cone and Howard Thurman.* Lanham, MD: University Press of America, 1989.

Stokes, Kenneth. *Faith is a Verb.* Mystic, CT: Twenty-Third Publications, 1992.

Stone, Howard W. *Theological Context for Pastoral Caregiving: Word in Deed.* New York: Haworth Pastoral Press, 1996.

Stroup, George W. *The Promise of Narrative Theology: Recovering the Gospel in the Church.* Atlanta: John Knox, 1981.

Surrey, Janet L. "Self-in-Relation: A Theory of Women's Development." Wellesley, MA: Wellesley Centers for Women, No. 13 (1985), http://www.wcwonline.org/pdf/previews/preview_13sc.pdf.

Taylor, Yuvall. *I was Born a Slave: An Anthology of Classic Slave Narratives.* Chicago: Lawrence Hill, 1999.

The Book of Discipline of the United Methodist Church 2000. Nashville: United Methodist Publishing, 2000.

This Holy Mystery: A United Methodist Understanding of Holy Communion. Nashville: General Board of Discipleship, 2003.

Thurman, Anne Spencer, ed., *For the Inward Journey: The Writings of Howard Thurman.* Richmond, IN: Friends United, 2002.

Thurman, Howard. *The Creative Encounter: An Interpretation of Religion and the Social Witness.* New York: Harper & Brothers, 1954.

______. *The Inward Journey.* Richmond, IN: Friends United, 1961.

______. *Mysticism and the Experience of Love.* Wallingford, PA: Pendle

Hill, 1961.

______. *Disciplines of the Spirit.* New York: Harper & Row, 1963.

______. *The Centering Moment.* New York: Harper & Row, 1969.

______. *Deep is the Hunger: Meditations for Apostles of Sensitiveness.* New York: Harper & Row, 1951. Reprint, Richmond, IN: Friends United, 1973.

______. "Mysticism and Social Change." Berkeley: Pacific School of Religion, 1978.

______. *With Head and Heart.* New York: Harcourt, Brace, Jovanovich, 1979.

______. "The Ground of Hope," *The Saturday Evening Post* 252, no. 1

(Jan/Feb 1980): 44-114.

______. "No Life Without War and Affliction." In *For the Inward Journey: The Writings of Howard Thurman*, ed. Anne Spencer Thurman, 59. Richmond, IN: Friends United, 2002.

Tillich, Paul. *Dynamics of Faith*. New York: Harper & Brothers, 1957.

Totten, Samuel. "Using Reader-Response Theory to Study Poetry about the Holocaust with High School Students." *Social Studies* 89, no. 1, (Jan/Feb 1998): 30-35.

VanKatwyk, Peter L. "Therapy Talk and Therapeutic Conversations: The Formation of Pastoral Counselor." *Journal of Pastoral Care & Counseling* 60, no. 4 (Winter 2006): 379-385.

Ware, Kallistos. "Symeon the New Theologian" in *The Study of Spirituality*, eds. Cheslyn Jones, G. Wainwright, & E. Yarnold, SJ, 235-241. New York: Oxford, 1986.

Warren, Heather A. J. L. Murray, and M. M. Best. "The Discipline and Habit of Theological Reflection." *Journal of Religion and Health* 41, no. 4 (Winter 2002): 323-331.

Watkins Ali, Carroll A. *Survival and Liberation: Pastoral Theology in the African American Context.* St. Louis: Chalice, 1999.

Wesley, John. "The Scripture Way of Salvation." In *John Wesley*, ed. Albert Outler, 271-282. New York: Oxford, 1964.

West, Cornel. "The Ignoble Paradox of Western Modernity." In Foreword to *Spirits of the Passage: The Transatlantic Slave Trade in the Seventeenth Century,* eds. Madeline Burnside and Rosemarie Robotham, 8. New York: Simon and Schuster, 1997, 7-8.

West, Cornel. *Race Matters.* Boston: Beacon, 1993.

Wheelis, Allen. *How People Change.* New York: Harper Colophon, 1973.

Whooley, Owen. "The Political Work of Narratives: A Dialogic Analysis of Two Slave Narratives." In *Narrative Inquiry* 16, no. 2 (2006): 295-318.

Willard, Dallas. *The Spirit of the Disciplines.* New York: Harper San Francisco, 1991.

Williams, Daniel Day. *The Spirit and the Forms of Love.* New York: Harper & Row, 1968.

Wilson, William Julius. *The Bridge Over the Racial Divide: Rising Inequality and Coalition Politics.* Berkeley: Univ. of California, 1999.

Wimberly, Edward. "The Family Context of Development: African American Families." In *Human Development and Faith: Life-Cycle Stages of Body, Mind, and Soul*, ed. Felicity B. Kelcourse, 111-125. St. Louis: Chalice, 2004.

Woodward, Kenneth L. "Is God Listening." *Newsweek* 129, no. 13 (March 31, 1997): 57-64.

Wulff, David M. *Psychology of Religion: Classic and Contemporary.* New York: John Wiley & Sons, 1997.

Wright, Conrad. *Walking Together.* Boston: Skinner House Books, 1989.

Ziegler, Phillip and Tobey Hiller. *Recreating Partnership.* New York: W. W. Norton, 2001.

Index

authority, 19, 56

awareness, 48, 50, 109, 117, 119–20, 126, 147, 167, 170, 179

B

Baird, Mary, 183

balance, 20, 48, 76, 94

Baldwin, 184

Baptist Church, 51, 115

beliefs, 3–4, 6, 9, 13, 19, 24–25, 28, 38–39, 64, 79–80, 90

belief systems, 6, 63–64, 90

believing, 29, 61, 63, 88

Bible, 24, 33, 102, 114, 116, 154

Black Pastoral Theology, 182

Black Theology, 183–84

blessings, 72, 101, 150

body, 25, 66, 105, 122, 127–28, 145, 156, 158, 187, 193

boundaries, 176

Broad Description of Faithing, 23

Buddha, 38, 52–53, 105, 152

Buddhism, 52, 104, 106, 149

C

capacity, 13, 17, 59, 61, 108, 115, 119, 136, 146, 150, 179

caring, 70, 130

Carlyle Fielding III, 191

Carse, James, 64

chanting, 102, 105, 126, 156

chaplains, 55–57, 133–34, 180

cheerleaders, 56, 95

child, 4, 26–27, 62, 108, 125, 161

children, 21, 33, 41, 92, 180

church, 4, 6–9, 27–29, 36, 51, 98, 103, 137, 143, 163, 166, 168, 174–77

church-hopping, 28

commandments, 8, 33, 124

commitment, 2, 66–67, 91, 97, 138–41, 175–77, 180

community, 2, 4, 26–27, 34, 38, 41, 51, 64, 99–100, 103, 173, 175–78, 180

compassion, 31, 40, 71, 100, 150, 156, 165

competence, 85, 146

Cone, James H., 191

confess, 121, 123

confession, 7, 185

confidence, 1–2, 4, 14, 19, 42–45, 49, 75–77, 87–88, 114–15, 159, 163

confident, 8, 12–14, 81, 85, 126

conflict avoidance, 165

conflicts, 20, 164–66, 168, 171

congregation, 7, 11, 28, 36, 44, 89, 125, 155, 167, 175, 177

connection, 157, 162–63

consciousness, 97, 105, 139–40, 164, 178, 187

contemplation, 9, 101, 161

context, 70, 116, 120, 155, 157, 189

conversations, 16, 27, 42, 50, 52, 61, 71, 73, 149, 172

convictions, 2–5, 9–10, 12–13, 16, 24, 52, 54, 64, 67, 77, 80

Cooper-Lewter, Nicholas, 90

coping strategy, 83

Counseling, 35, 183, 185, 187, 189–90, 192
  professional, 151

counseling theory, 68

couples, 75, 121, 162

family, 12, 15–17, 20–21, 31–32, 41, 45, 51–52, 55, 62–63, 80, 86, 92–93, 153

family system, 20–21

feelings, 17, 21, 38–39, 86, 111, 113, 165, 172–73

Feminism, 184

Feminist, 184, 188

Feminist Theory in Pastoral Theology, 188

Fisk, Alfred, 175

Fluker, Walter, 118

forgiveness, 100, 165

Fowler, 19, 184

framework, 111, 123, 149, 176, 179

Frankl, Victor, 131

freedom, 64, 77, 188

FreeThinking Mystics, 107, 189

friendships, 1, 93–94

the fruit of the spirit, 39

fruits, 37, 39–41, 43

G

generations, 12, 20, 31, 50, 176

gifts, 12, 17–18, 25, 41, 43, 55, 92, 101

giving, 22, 102, 120–21, 143–44, 154

goals, 22, 81, 85–86, 91, 139–41, 156, 171

  spiritual, 140, 143, 148

God, 7–8, 21, 30–33, 36, 81–82, 85–86, 103–4, 108–10, 116, 118–19, 136, 156–58, 164, 171–73, 180–81, 185, 188–91

grace, 3, 92, 158, 176–77

gratitude, 58, 66, 71, 125, 158, 162

ground, 59, 65, 75, 96, 126, 160

group, 12, 42, 47, 55, 112, 167, 169, 177–79

Inward Journey, 39, 117, 119, 191–92

J

Jarena Lee, 186–87

Jesus, 38, 183

journal, 9, 69–71, 106, 173, 187, 190–91

journaling, 69–71, 171–73

journey, 18, 22, 30–31, 46, 52, 55, 88, 91, 97, 106, 108

  spiritual, 13, 53, 102, 141, 155, 174

joy, 3, 7, 15, 22, 40, 66, 145, 162

K

Kahlil Gibran, 39

knowing, 9, 12, 17, 30–31, 35–36, 39, 74, 87, 90, 114, 117, 156, 159

knowledge, 13, 26, 33, 38–39, 64, 74, 89–90, 115, 118, 121

L

language, 105, 114, 140, 156, 169

  non-God, 104

leadership, 20, 178

learning, 2–3, 10, 42, 44, 55–57, 60, 77, 97–98, 114, 143, 152

Liberation, 33, 112, 191, 193

Life-Cycle Stages, 187, 193

life of faith, 10–11, 14, 17–18, 23–24, 37, 39, 41, 43–45, 85–86, 89, 97–98, 180, 183

life's struggles, 79

lifestyle, 67, 130, 145, 152

listening, 6, 47, 49–50, 98, 106, 161, 163, 166, 169, 181, 186

love, 37, 40–41, 74, 77, 86–87, 109–10, 118–25, 132, 135, 150–51, 156–57, 176–77, 192–93

M

marriage, 13, 93, 121

Martin Luther King, 184

meaning, 6, 16, 19, 22, 28–29, 39, 55–56, 110, 114, 117, 131–32

Meaning of Sensitiveness, 118

meditating, 80, 103, 106, 126, 161

meditation, 9, 18, 47, 65, 67, 102, 127, 156

memories, 33–36, 38–39, 42, 61, 88, 131, 161

mental health, 72, 151, 186

mentors, 58, 97–98

  spiritual, 4, 40, 59

Mentors, Faith, 60, 92

milestones, 18, 92

Miller-McLemore, Bonnie J., 184, 188

mind, 3, 60, 62, 69–70, 75–76, 82, 103, 105–6, 127–29, 132, 139–40, 142, 172–73, 178, 180

mindfulness, 113, 127, 180

minister, 6–7, 28–29, 51, 56, 97–98, 108, 155, 169, 180

ministry, 36–37, 56, 92, 97, 133, 150, 163, 190

monastics, 82

money, 68, 88, 143–44, 148

music, 36, 47–48, 127

mystical experience, 2, 104, 106, 108, 110–11, 113, 116, 119–20, 125, 174

mysticism, 2, 103–4, 106–10, 114, 117–18, 179, 182, 188, 192

mystics, 103–7, 109–11, 113–14, 117, 120, 123, 126, 191

Thurman, Howard, 22, 108–9, 148, 183–84, 189, 191–92

traditions, 5, 51–53, 105–7, 114, 116–17, 119, 140, 152, 156

transcendence, 17, 50, 180

transcendent, 50, 68, 82, 104, 106, 112–13, 118–19, 155, 159

transformation, 24, 53, 63, 174

trials, 35–36, 77, 123, 180

tribulations, 36

trust, 4–5, 9, 12–13, 15–17, 19, 37–38, 75, 77, 86–90, 92, 113–14, 136, 138, 149–50

trusting, 2–3, 8, 12, 31, 36–38, 86–88, 91, 136, 150, 165, 173

truth, 5, 33, 49, 53, 63–64, 94, 110–11, 136, 141, 156, 176

U

ultimate, 110, 117, 173

ultimate concern, 114

understanding, 25–27, 29, 108, 110, 118, 121, 123, 125, 150, 154, 161–62, 164

Unitarian Universalism, 52, 111, 130, 155

Unitarian Universalist (UU), 6, 11, 46, 107, 116, 156, 163, 174

unity, 29, 112, 126, 171, 177, 179

universe, 32, 38, 87–88, 90, 125, 128, 155, 157–58, 160, 164, 177, 179

V

values, 4, 9–10, 12, 94, 100, 115, 143, 185

vicissitudes, 17, 35–36, 71, 137

vision, 15, 22–23, 34, 86, 132, 174, 176

W

wealth, 52–54